America's Choice:
high skills or low wages!

The Report of

The Commission on the Skills of the American Workforce

June 1990

NATIONAL
CENTER
ON
EDUCATION
AND THE
ECONOMY

The National Center on Education and the Economy

The National Center on Education and the Economy is a not-for-profit organization created to develop proposals for building the world class education and training system that the United States must have if it is to have a world class economy. The Center engages in policy analysis and development and works collaboratively with others at local, state and national levels to advance its proposals in the policy arena.

National Center on Education
    and the Economy
39 State Street
Suite 500
Rochester, New York 14614
716/546-7620
FAX: 716/546-3145

COMMISSION ON THE SKILLS OF THE AMERICAN WORKFORCE

Ira C. Magaziner, *Chair*
President
SJS, Inc.

William E. Brock, *Co-Chair*
Senior Partner
The Brock Group
Former Secretary
U.S. Department of Labor

Ray Marshall, *Co-Chair*
Chair in Economics and Public Affairs
L.B.J. School of Public Affairs
University of Texas at Austin
Former Secretary
U.S. Department of Labor

Robert M. Atkinson
Director of Academic Programs
School of Business and Industry
Florida A & M University

Owen Bieber
President
United Automobile Workers

Edward J. Carlough
General President
Sheet Metal Workers' International
  Association

Anthony P. Carnevale
Vice President of National Affairs
  and Chief Economist
American Society for Training
  and Development

Paul J. Choquette, Jr.
President and Chief Executive Officer
Gilbane Building Company

Richard Cohon
President
C. N. Burman Company

Badi G. Foster
President
AEtna Institute for Corporate Education

Thomas Gonzales
Chancellor
Seattle Community College District VI

Rear Admiral W. J. Holland, Jr., USN (Retired)
President
Educational Foundation
Armed Forces Communications and
  Education Association

James R. Houghton
Chairman of the Board and
  Chief Executive Officer
Corning Incorporated

James B. Hunt, Jr.
Partner
Poyner & Spruill
Former Governor
State of North Carolina

John R. Hurley
Vice President and Director
Corporate Training and Educational
  Resources
The Chase Manhattan Bank

John E. Jacob
President and Chief Executive Officer
National Urban League, Inc.

Thomas H. Kean
President
Drew University
Former Governor
State of New Jersey

William H. Kolberg
President
National Alliance of Business

William Lucy
International Secretary/Treasurer
American Federation of State,
County and Municipal Employees, AFL-CIO

Margaret L.A. MacVicar
Dean for Undergraduate Education
and Professor
Massachusetts Institute of Technology

Eleanor Holmes Norton
Professor of Law
Georgetown University Law Center
Former Chairwoman of the Equal
Employment Opportunity Commission

Karen Nussbaum
Executive Director
9to5, National Association of
Working Women

Peter J. Pestillo
Vice President
Corporate Relations and Diversified
Businesses
Ford Motor Company

Philip H. Power
Chairman
Suburban Communications Corporation

Lauren B. Resnick
Director
Learning Research and Development Center
University of Pittsburgh

Kjell-Jon Rye
Teacher
Bellevue (WA) Public Schools

Howard D. Samuel
President
Industrial Union Department
AFL-CIO

John Sculley
Chairman, President and
Chief Executive Officer
Apple Computer, Inc.

William J. Spring
Vice President
District Community Affairs
Federal Reserve Bank of Boston

Anthony J. Trujillo
Superintendent
Sweetwater Union (CA) High School District

Marc S. Tucker
President
National Center on Education
and the Economy

Laura D'Andrea Tyson
Director of Research
Berkeley Roundtable on the
International Economy
University of California at Berkeley

Kay R. Whitmore
Chairman, President, and
Chief Executive Officer
Eastman Kodak Company

Alan L. Wurtzel
Chairman of the Board
Circuit City Stores, Inc.

Signatories

Ira C. Magaziner, *Chair*

William E. Brock, *Co-Chair*

Ray Marshall, *Co-Chair*

Robert M. Atkinson

Owen Bieber

Edward J. Carlough

Anthony P. Carnevale

Paul J. Choquette, Jr.

Richard Cohon

Badi G. Foster

Thomas Gonzales

W. J. Holland, Jr.

James R. Houghton

James B. Hunt, Jr.

John R. Hurley

John E. Jacob

Thomas H. Kean

William H. Kolberg

William Lucy

Margaret L. A. MacVicar

Eleanor Holmes Norton

Karen Nussbaum

Peter J. Pestillo

Philip H. Power

Lauren B. Resnick

Kjell-Jon Rye

John Sculley

Anthony J. Trujillo

Marc S. Tucker

Alan L. Wurtzel

Howard D. Samuel

William J. Spring

Laura D'Andrea Tyson

Kay R. Whitmore

TABLE OF CONTENTS

Executive Summary

EXECUTIVE SUMMARY

The Problem

Since 1969, real average weekly earnings in the United States have fallen by more than 12 percent. This burden has been shared unequally. The incomes of our top 30 percent of earners increased while those of the other 70 percent spiraled downward.

In many families, it now takes two people working to make ends meet, where one was sufficient in the past.

The United States is in the midst of the second longest economic expansion in its history. But that expansion is built largely on the fact that 50 percent of our population is employed compared with 40 percent in 1973. Forty million new jobs were created as the 'baby boom' generation reached working age, and more women entered the workforce. More of us have been working so we produced more.

However, workforce growth will slow dramatically in the 1990's. We can no longer grow substantially just by adding new workers.

The key to maintaining, to say nothing of improving, our standard of living is productivity growth — more products and services from every member of the workforce.

But, during the past two decades, our productivity growth has slowed to a crawl. It now takes nearly three years to achieve the same productivity improvement we used to achieve in one year.

If productivity continues to falter, we can expect one of two futures. Either the top 30 percent of our population will grow wealthier while the bottom 70 percent becomes progressively poorer or we all slide into relative poverty together.

The Task

To ensure a more prosperous future, we must improve productivity and our competitive position. We cannot simply do this by using better machinery, because low wage countries can now use the same machines and can still sell their products more cheaply than we can.

The key to productivity improvement for a high wage nation lies in the third industrial revolution now taking place in the world. The steam engine and electric motor drove the first two industrial revolutions, causing profound changes in work organization. This boosted productivity, quality and living standards dramatically. The creation of the modern factory in the 1800's and mass production in the 1900's followed these technology breakthroughs.

The advent of the computer, high speed communication and universal education are heralding a third industrial revolution, a revolution the key feature of which is high performance work organization.

The Organization Of Work In America

The organization of America's workplaces today is largely modeled after the system of mass manufacture pioneered during the early 1900's. The premise is simple: Break complex jobs into a myriad of simple rote tasks, which the worker then repeats with machine-like efficiency.

The system is managed by a small group of educated planners and supervisors who do the thinking for the organization. They plan strategy, implement changes, motivate the workers and solve problems. Extensive administrative procedures allow managers to keep control of a large number of workers. This form of work organization is often referred to as the 'Taylor' model.

Most employees under this model need not be educated. It is far more important that they be reliable, steady and willing to follow directions.

But in the world's best companies, new high performance work organizations are replacing this 'Taylor' method. These companies are using a new approach to unleash major advances in productivity, quality, variety and speed of new product introductions.

Mass production methods will continue to produce high volume, inexpensive goods and services for a long time to come. But what the world is prepared to pay high prices and high wages for now is quality, variety and responsiveness to changing consumer tastes, the very qualities that the new methods of organizing work make possible.

'Tayloristic' methods are not well suited to these goals. Firms struggling to apply the traditional methods of work organization to more complex technologies, more frequent product introductions, increased quality requirements and proliferating product variety often create cumbersome and inefficient bureaucracies.

The new high performance forms of work organization operate very differently. Rather than increasing bureaucracy, they reduce it by giving front-line workers more responsibility. Workers are asked to use judgment and make decisions. Management layers disappear as front-line workers assume responsibility for many of the tasks — from quality control to production scheduling — that others used to do.

Work organizations like these require large investments in training. Workers' pay levels often rise to reflect their greater qualifications and responsibilities. But the productivity and quality gains more than offset the costs to the company of higher wages and skills development.

Despite these advantages, 95 percent of American companies still cling to old forms of work organization.

Is There A Skills Shortage In The United States?

Because most American employers organize work in a way that does not require high skills, they report no shortage of people who have such skills and foresee no such shortage. With some exceptions, the education and skill levels of American workers roughly match the demands of their jobs.

Our research did reveal a wide range of concerns covered under the blanket term of 'skills.' While businesses everywhere complained about the quality of their applicants, few talked about the kinds of skills acquired in school. The primary concern of more than 80 percent of employers was finding workers with a good work ethic and appropriate social behavior: 'reliable,' 'a good attitude,' 'a pleasant appearance,' 'a good personality.'

Most employers we interviewed do not expect their skill requirements to change. Despite the widespread presumption that advancing technology and the evolving service economy will create jobs demanding higher skills, only five percent of employers were concerned about a skills shortage. These were mainly large manufacturers, financial service organizations and communications companies.

The reason we have no skills shortage today is that we are using a turn-of-the-century work organization. If we want to compete more effectively in the global economy, we will have to move to a high productivity work organization.

How We Prepare Our Front-Line Workers For Work

More than 70 percent of the jobs in America will not require a college education by the year 2000. These jobs are the backbone of our economy, and the productivity of workers in these jobs will make or break our economic future.

No nation has produced a highly qualified technical workforce without first providing its workers with a strong general education. But our children rank at the bottom on most international tests — behind children in Europe and East Asia, even behind children in some newly industrialized countries.

More than any other country in the world, the United States believes that natural ability, rather than effort, explains achievement. The tragedy is that we communicate to millions of students every year, especially to low-income and minority students, that we do not believe that they have what it takes to learn. They then live up to our expectations, despite the evidence that they can meet very high performance standards under the right conditions.

Unlike virtually all of our leading competitors, we have no national system capable of setting high academic standards for the non-college bound or of assessing their achievement against those standards.

America may have the worst school-to-work transition system of any advanced industrial country. Students who know few adults to help them get their first job are left to sink or swim.

Only eight percent of our front-line workers receive any formal training once on the job, and this is usually limited to orientation for new hires or short courses on team building or safety.

The American post-secondary education and training system was never designed to meet the needs of our front-line workers. The system is a combination of education programs for full-time college students and short term training for the severely disadvantaged, and can be difficult to access. Because employers have not set training standards, few students can be sure that there is a market for the courses they pursue. Education is rarely connected to training and both are rarely connected to an effective job service function.

Another Way

While the foreign nations we studied differ in economy and culture, they share an approach to the education and training of their workers and to high productivity work organization.

- They insist that virtually all of their students reach a high educational standard. We do not.

- They provide 'professionalized' education to non-college bound students to prepare them for their trades and to ease their school-to-work transition. We do not.

- They operate comprehensive labor market systems which combine training, labor market information, job search and income maintenance for the unemployed. We do not.

- They support company based training through general revenue or payroll tax based financing schemes. We do not.

- They have national consensus on the importance of moving to high productivity forms of work organization and building high wage economies. We do not.

Our approaches have served us well in the past. They will not serve us well in the future.

The Choice

Americans are unwittingly making a choice. It is a choice that most of us would probably not make were we aware of its consequences. Yet every day, that choice is becoming more difficult to reverse. It is a choice which undermines the American dream of economic opportunity for all. It is a choice that will lead to an America where 30 percent of our people may do well — at least for awhile — but the other 70 percent will see their dreams slip away.

The choice that America faces is a choice between high skills and low wages. Gradually, silently, we are choosing low wages.

We still have time to make the other choice — one that will lead us to a more prosperous future. To make this choice, we must fundamentally change our approach to work and education.

1. Problem: Two factors stand in the way of producing a highly educated workforce: We lack a clear standard of achievement and few students are motivated to work hard in school. One reason that students going right to work after school have little motivation to study hard is that they see little or no relationship between how well they do in school and what kind of job they can get after school. Other advanced industrial nations have stringent performance standards that virtually all students must meet at about age 16 and that directly affect their employment prospects.

Recommendation: *A new educational performance standard should be set for all students, to be met by age 16. This standard should be established nationally and benchmarked to the highest in the world.*

We propose that all American students meet a national standard of educational excellence by age 16, or soon thereafter. Students passing a series of performance based assessments that incorporate the standard would be awarded a Certificate of Initial Mastery.

Possession of the Certificate of Initial Mastery would qualify the student to choose among going to work, entering a college preparatory program or studying for a Technical and Professional Certificate, described below.

Creation of the Certificate of Initial Mastery standard would require a new approach to student performance assessment. We recommend the creation of new performance based examinations for which students can explicitly prepare. The assessment system would provide multiple opportunities for success rather than a single high stakes moment of possible failure. Most important, the examination, though set at a very high standard, is not intended as a sorting mechanism on the pattern of virtually all the major tests now in use. Our goal is to set a tough standard that almost everyone will reach, although not all at the same time.

Once created, this system would establish objective standards for students and educators, motivate students and give employers an objective means to evaluate the accomplishments of students.

2. Problem: More than 20 percent of our students drop out of high school — almost 50 percent in many of our inner cities. These dropouts go on to make up more than one third of our front-line workforce. Turning our backs on those dropouts, as we do now, is tantamount to turning our backs on our future workforce.

Recommendation: *The states should take responsibility for assuring that virtually all students achieve the Certificate of Initial Mastery. Through the new local Employment and Training Boards, states, with federal assistance, should create and fund alternative learning environments for those who cannot attain the Certificate of Initial Mastery in regular schools.*

All students should be guaranteed the educational attention necessary to attain the Certificate of Initial Mastery by age 16, or as soon as possible thereafter. Youth Centers should be established to enroll school dropouts and help them reach that standard.

Federal, state and local funds should be raised or reallocated to finance these dropout recovery programs. Once the Youth Centers are created, children should not be permitted to work before the age of 18 unless they have attained the Certificate of Initial Mastery or are enrolled in a program to attain it.

3. Problem: Other industrial nations have multi-year career-oriented educational programs that prepare students to operate at a professional level in the workplace. Graduates of these programs have the skills to hit the ground running when they get their first full-time job at age 19 or 20. America prepares only a tiny fraction of its non-college bound students for work. As a result, most flounder in the labor market, moving from low paying job to low paying job until their mid-twenties, never being seriously trained.

Recommendation: *A comprehensive system of Technical and Professional Certificates and associate's degrees should be created for the majority of our students and adult workers who do not pursue a baccalaureate degree.*

Technical and Professional Certificates would be offered across the entire range of service and manufacturing occupations. A student could earn the entry-level occupation specific certificate after completing a two- to four-year program of combined work and study, depending upon the field. A sequence of advanced certificates, attesting to mastery of more complex skills, would be available and could be obtained throughout one's career.

The Secretary of Labor should convene national committees of business, labor, education and public representatives to define certification standards for two- to four-year programs of professional preparation in a broad range of occupations. These programs should combine general education with specific occupational skills and should include a significant work component.

Students could pursue these programs at a wide variety of institutions accredited to offer them, including high schools, community colleges and proprietary schools. The system should be designed to make it possible for students to move easily between the Certificate programs and college.

A means should be established to ensure that all students can receive financing to pursue these programs.

4. Problem: The vast majority of American employers are not moving to high performance work organizations, nor are they investing to train their non-managerial employees for these new work organizations. The movement to high performance work organizations is more widespread in other nations, and training of front-line workers, funded in part by national assessments on employers or general public revenues, is commonplace.

Recommendation: *All employers should be given incentives and assistance to invest in the further education and training of their workers and to pursue high productivity forms of work organization.*

We propose a system whereby all employers will invest at least one percent of their payroll for the education and training of their workers. Those who do not wish to participate would contribute the one percent to a general training fund, to be used by states to upgrade worker skills. We further recommend that public technical assistance be provided to companies, particularly small businesses, to assist them in moving to higher performance work organizations.

5. Problem: The United States is not well organized to provide the highly skilled workers needed to support the emerging high performance work organizations. Public policy on worker training has been largely passive, except for the needs of a small portion of the severely disadvantaged population. The training system is fragmented with respect to policies, administration and service delivery.

Recommendation: *A system of Employment and Training Boards should be established by Federal and state governments, together with local leadership, to organize and oversee the new school-to-work transition programs and training systems we propose.*

We envision a new, more comprehensive system where skills development and upgrading for the majority of our workers becomes a central aim of public policy.

The key to accomplishing these goals is finding a way to enable the leaders of our communities to take responsibility for building a comprehensive system that meets their needs. The local Employment and Training Boards for each major labor market would:

- Take responsibility for the school-to-work and Youth Center-to-work transition for young people.

- Manage and oversee the Youth Centers.

- Manage and oversee a 'second chance' system for adults seeking the Certificate of Initial Mastery.

- Manage and oversee the system for awarding Technical and Professional Certificates at the local level.

- Manage a labor market information system.

- Manage and oversee the job service.

- Coordinate existing programs.

The states would need to create a parallel structure to support the local Boards, coordinate statewide functions and establish state standards for their operation.

In Conclusion

America is headed toward an economic cliff. We will no longer be able to put a higher proportion of our people to work to generate economic growth. If basic changes are not made, real wages will continue to fall, especially for the majority who do not graduate from four-year colleges. The gap between economic 'haves' and 'have nots' will widen still further and social tensions will deepen.

Our recommendations provide an alternative for America. We do not pretend that this vision will be easily accepted or quickly implemented. But we also cannot pretend that the status quo is an option. It is no longer possible to be a high wage, low skill nation. We have choices to make:

- Do we continue to define educational success as 'time in the seat,' or choose a new system that focuses on the demonstrated achievement of high standards?

- Do we continue to provide little incentive for non-college bound students to study hard and take tough subjects, or choose a system that will reward real effort with better pay and better jobs?

- Do we continue to turn our backs on America's school dropouts, or choose to take responsibility for educating them?

- Do we continue to provide unskilled workers for unskilled jobs, or train skilled workers and give companies incentives to deploy them in high performance work organizations?

- Do we continue in most companies to limit training to a select handful of managers and professionals, or choose to provide training to front-line workers as well?

- Do we cling to a public employment and training system fragmented by institutional barriers, muddled by overlapping bureaucracies and operating at the margins of the labor market, or do we choose a unified system that addresses itself to a majority of workers?

- Do we continue to remain indifferent to the low wage path being chosen by many companies, or do we provide incentives for high productivity choices?

Taken together, the Commission's recommendations provide the framework for developing a high quality American education and training system, closely linked to high performance work organizations. The system we propose provides a uniquely American solution. Boldly executed, it has the potential not simply to put us on an equal footing with our competitors, but to allow us to leap ahead, to build the world's premier workforce. In so doing, we will create a formidable competitive advantage.

The status quo is not an option. The choice we have is to become a nation of high skills or one of low wages.

The choice is ours. It should be clear. It must be made.

Preface

PREFACE

The three of us who chair this Commission have grown increasingly uneasy as we have watched Singapore, Taiwan and Korea grow from run-down Third World outposts to world premier exporters; as Germany, with one quarter of our population, almost equaled us in exports; as Japan became the world's economic juggernaut; and, as America became the world's biggest borrower.

As all this happened, we heard the excuses: The countries we beat in the Second World War are simply regaining their former place in the world. The Europeans and the Japanese are exploiting their low wages. Our competitors are class-ridden countries.

The truth is otherwise: Our former adversaries are doing far better in relation to us than they did before the war. A dozen nations now pay wages above ours. Our distribution of income is more skewed than any of our major competitors and our poverty rate is much higher.

Our education statistics are as disappointing as our trade statistics. Our children rank at the bottom on most international tests — behind children in Europe and East Asia. Again, we heard the excuses: They have elite systems, but we educate everyone. They compare a small number of their best to our much larger average.

The facts are otherwise: Many of the countries with the highest test scores have more of their students in school than we do.

The apologists say it is unfair to compare their scores to ours because we must educate a diverse population, while their student bodies are homogeneous. This is the most disturbing excuse of all. Do we really believe that Black, Hispanic and immigrant children can't be educated to the same standard as Whites? Whites are a declining percentage of our youth. If we bow to this excuse, we are giving up on America.

But isn't this America-bashing? Don't we have firms in America as competitive as any in the world? Don't we have schools as good as those in any country? Isn't it true that we are in the midst of one of the longest economic expansions this country has ever had?

Sure, but we are not facing the facts about our future.

What we are facing is an economic cliff of sorts. And the front-line working people of America are about to fall off it.

From the 1950's to the 1970's, America's productivity grew at a healthy pace. The nation was getting richer, and workers lived better on what they earned.

Since then, the rate of increase in productivity has dropped dramatically. The distribution of income in the United States has been worsening. Those with college degrees are prospering, but the front-line workers have seen the buying power of their paychecks shrink year after year.

To be sure, the economy has grown. But that growth came from the fact that more of us have been working. During the 1980's a higher percentage of Americans were working than at any time in this century. The 'baby boom' generation came into the workforce and many women went to work to maintain family incomes at their former levels.

In addition, the country has been borrowing at unprecedented levels to maintain national income. We underinvested in our infrastructure and allowed it to deteriorate. As a result, many of us are living as well as we did, but we are living on borrowed money and borrowed time.

What happens now? In the future, we cannot grow our economy by putting more people to work, as we have done for 30 years. Fewer people are entering the workforce, and fewer still will enter in the years ahead. We must grow by having every American worker produce more. If we don't, our incomes will go into a free fall with no end in sight.

That is the economic cliff we face.

To avoid falling off, many policy changes are needed, but one thing is certain: we must work more productively and be more competitive. We cannot do this simply by using better machinery, because low wage countries can now use the same machines and still sell their products more cheaply than we can.

We can do this only by mobilizing our most vital asset, the skills of our people — not just the 30 percent who will graduate from college, but the front-line workers, the people who serve as bank tellers, farm workers, truck drivers, retail clerks, data entry operators, laborers and factory workers.

We can do this only by reorganizing the way we work in our stores and factories, in our warehouses and insurance offices, and in our government agencies and hospitals. We can give much more responsibility to our front-line workers, educate them well and train them to do more highly skilled jobs.

By doing this, we streamline work. Many fewer supervisors, fewer quality checkers, fewer production schedulers and fewer maintenance people are needed, so organizations become more efficient. Because they are more efficient, they can sell more. Because they can sell more, they can expand. Because they can expand, they can employ more people. Although each operation requires fewer people, society as a whole can increase employment and wages can go up.

Our most formidable international competitors are doing just this. For the most part, we are not.

We still have a robust economy. Some of our firms are among the best run in the world. They learned how to organize for high productivity. If many more do so, and we make the required investment in skills for our front-line workers, this country will have a very bright future. If not, our incomes will decline at an accelerated pace.

This is our choice: high skills or low wages.

Bill Brock
Co-Chair

Ira C. Magaziner
Chair

Ray Marshall
Co-Chair

The Report

1

THE PROBLEM

Over the past two decades, our productivity growth has slowed to a crawl, our incomes have stagnated and the wage gap has widened between our nation's educational 'haves' and 'have nots.'

From 1960 to 1973, American private, nonagricultural workers each produced an average of 2.9 percent more every year than the year before. Since 1973, it has taken nearly three years to achieve the same productivity improvement gained in one pre-1973 year.

Our economy has grown because we now have 50 percent of our people working instead of 40 percent as in 1973. We added 40 million new jobs. More of us have been working, so we have produced more.

Because our economic growth has not come from improved productivity, however, our wages have not improved. In fact, real average weekly earnings have dropped more than 12 percent since 1969.

These hardships have not been borne equally by all Americans:

• The highest earning 30 percent of American families increased their share of national income from 54 percent in 1967 to 58 percent in 1987, while the bottom 70 percent have been losing ground.

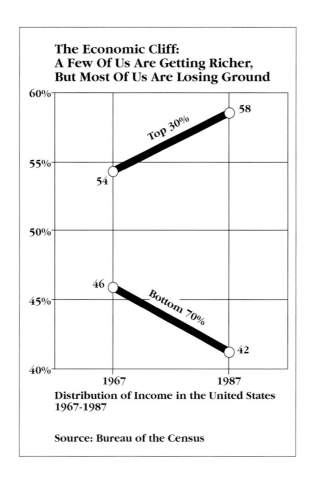

**The Economic Cliff:
A Few Of Us Are Getting Richer,
But Most Of Us Are Losing Ground**

**Distribution of Income in the United States
1967-1987**

Source: Bureau of the Census

- Over the past 15 years, the earnings gap between white collar professionals and skilled tradespeople has gone from two percent to 37 percent; the gap between professionals and clerical workers has gone from 47 percent to 86 percent.

- Over the past decade, earnings of college-educated males age 24 to 34 increased by 10 percent. Earnings of those with only high-school diplomas declined by nine percent. And those in the workforce who do not hold high-school diplomas saw their real incomes drop by 12 percent.

- Over 60 percent of White families have incomes over $25,000 per year, compared with only 49 percent of Hispanic families and 36 percent of Black families. The poverty rate for Black families is nearly three times that for Whites, and the gap has been widening.

- One in five American children — one third of our future front-line workforce — is born into poverty.

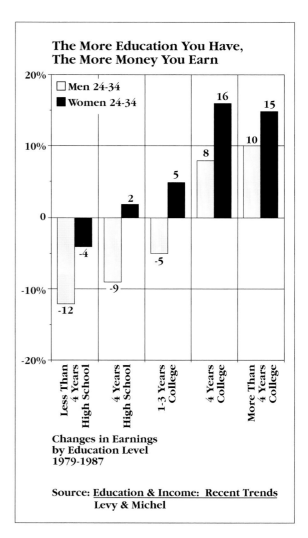

The More Education You Have, The More Money You Earn

□ Men 24-34
■ Women 24-34

Changes in Earnings by Education Level 1979-1987

Source: Education & Income: Recent Trends
Levy & Michel

What The Future Holds

Our population in the 1990's is likely to grow at about eight percent, a slower rate than for any period since the 1950's. This compares to a 1970's growth rate of 20 percent and a 1980's rate of 11 percent. Over 40 percent of new workforce entrants will be minorities and immigrants, groups which are at disproportionately low income levels today.

We can no longer depend upon more people working to give us economic growth. If productivity continues to falter, and real wages decline, we can expect one of two futures. Either the top 30 percent of our population grows wealthier while the bottom 70 percent becomes progressively poorer or we may all slide into relative poverty together.

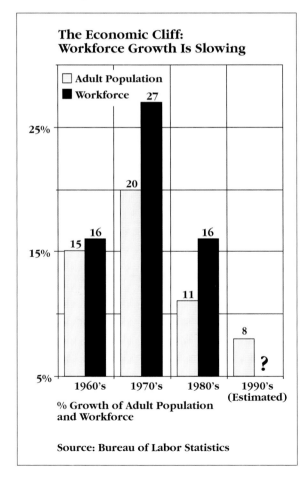

The Economic Cliff: Workforce Growth Is Slowing

□ Adult Population
■ Workforce

% Growth of Adult Population and Workforce

Source: Bureau of Labor Statistics

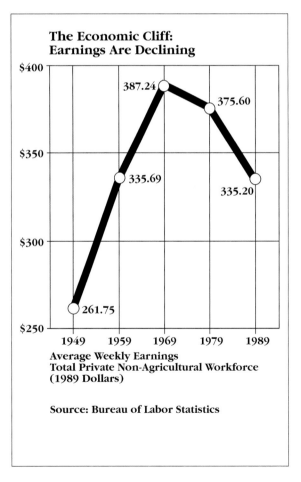

The Economic Cliff: Earnings Are Declining

Average Weekly Earnings
Total Private Non-Agricultural Workforce
(1989 Dollars)

Source: Bureau of Labor Statistics

To choose a more prosperous future, we must improve productivity. As we shall see, this will require major changes in the way we organize our workplaces, and a major investment in the skills of our people.

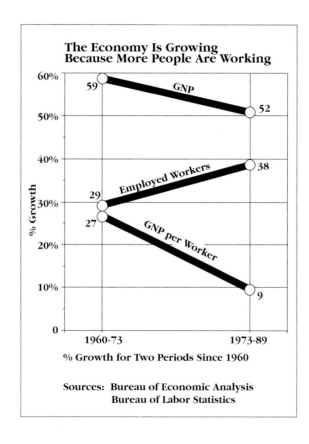

The Economy Is Growing Because More People Are Working

GNP

Employed Workers

GNP per Worker

% Growth

1960-73   1973-89

% Growth for Two Periods Since 1960

Sources: Bureau of Economic Analysis
Bureau of Labor Statistics

2

IS THERE A SKILLS SHORTAGE?

A front-page series in *The New York Times* last September foretold an impending crisis in our national workforce. David Kearns, Chairman of Xerox Corporation, described "the makings of a national disaster." Former Chairman of Procter & Gamble Brad Butler predicted the creation of "a Third World within our country." And James Burke, Chief Executive Officer of Johnson & Johnson, lamented "the American dream turned nightmare."

Strong language is not new to the debate over the American skills crisis. Since the release of the *Workforce 2000* report in 1987, the attention of our nation's business and education communities, and increasingly of our governments, has focused on the problem of the mismatch of skills to jobs.

Companies are sounding the alarm. Telephone sales jobs are going begging in Boston because MCI cannot find qualified workers; textile workers are no longer able to operate their computerized machines; and aircraft manufacturers in California have teamed up out of necessity to train employees. Companies such as New York Tele-phone report hiring frustrations of epic proportions — 57,000 applicants had to be tested to find 2,100 who were qualified to fill entry level technical jobs.

The cry from America's board rooms, education think tanks and government officials is two-fold: America's workers are ill-equipped to meet employers' current needs and ill-prepared for the rapidly ap-proaching high technology, service-oriented future.

So why, given the scope of the existing debate, launch yet another study of America's skills crisis? It was our purpose to go back and examine the skills issue from the bottom up, to propose solutions by grappling with the problem's underlying causes.

This required visiting hundreds of American firms in all sectors of the economy and interviewing thousands of employers, personnel managers, production supervisors and workers. The goal of our inquiry was to understand what American workers are doing — what their jobs demand, what their employers expect of them and how these expectations are likely to change in the future.

... why, given the scope of the existing debate, launch yet another study of America's skills crisis? It was our purpose to go back and examine the skills issue from the bottom up, to [grapple] with the problem's underlying causes.

The primary concern of more than 80 percent of employers is finding workers with a good work ethic and appropriate social behavior — 'reliable,' 'a good attitude,' 'a pleasant appearance,' 'a good personality.'

We did not anticipate what we found. The picture we uncovered was of a skills shortage, but one much more subtle and complex, and ultimately more discomforting, than that reflected in the public debate.

Our research revealed a wide range of concerns covered under the blanket term of 'skills.' While businesses everywhere complain about the quality of their applicants, few refer to the kinds of skills acquired in school. The primary concern of more than 80 percent of employers is finding workers with a good work ethic and appropriate social behavior — 'reliable,' 'a good attitude,' 'a pleasant appearance,' 'a good personality.'

Although a few managers are worried about literacy and basic math skills, education levels rarely seem a concern. Employers do not complain about an inability to do algebra or write essays, though some are frustrated that a large number of their employees do not possess the elementary capability to read a production schedule or follow an instruction card.

Many employers require a high-school diploma for all new hires, yet very few believe that the diploma indicates educational achievement. More than 90 percent view the diploma as a sign of the applicant's reliability and staying power, proof only that they did not drop out.

Less than 30 percent of our sample firms are concerned about the labor market predictions of *Workforce 2000: Work and Workers for the 21st Century* — that women, minorities and immigrants will make up the vast majority of new entrants to the workforce in the 1990's and jobs requiring higher skills will grow faster than low skill jobs. Few of these firms are worried about skills. Their focus is on providing day care for workers' children or English as a Second Language classes.

A few of the employers surveyed (15 percent) mentioned occupation-specific shortages. The most commonly reported shortages are for workers in the traditional craft apprentice trades, like skilled construction or manufacturing, and in such traditionally female occupations as skilled secretaries, clerks and nurses.

These shortages can be largely attributed to changes in the relative earning potential of these workers. Men and women who ordinarily would have gone into skilled non-college jobs that require substantial preparation have chosen to attend college to take advantage of the higher wages offered to college graduates.

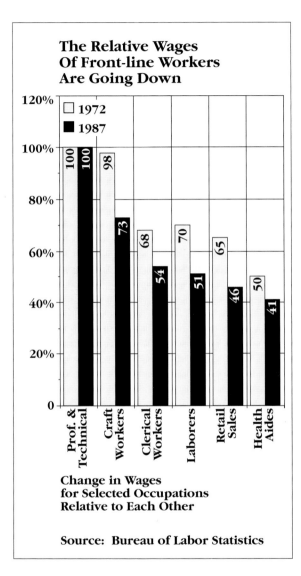

**The Relative Wages
Of Front-line Workers
Are Going Down**

□ 1972
■ 1987

	Prof. & Technical	Craft Workers	Clerical Workers	Laborers	Retail Sales	Health Aides
1972	100	98	68	70	65	50
1987	100	73	54	51	46	41

**Change in Wages
for Selected Occupations
Relative to Each Other**

Source: Bureau of Labor Statistics

Perhaps even more interesting than the absence of an obvious skills gap was the lack of any expectation among the majority of employers that their skill requirements would be changing. Despite the widespread presumption that advancing technology and the evolving service economy would create jobs demanding higher skills, only five percent of employers are concerned about growing educational skill needs. These were mainly large manufacturers, financial service organizations and communications firms.

To sum up, in our survey of employers across America, we found:

- Only five percent of employers feel that education and skill requirements are increasing significantly.

- More than 80 percent of employers express concern about 'skills' shortages, but they generally mean a good work ethic and social skills.

- Employers who think that education levels are insufficient usually refer to illiteracy and a lack of basic math skills.

- Only 15 percent of employers report difficulty finding workers with the appropriate occupational skills. These shortages are generally in chronically underpaid 'women's' occupations and traditional craft trades.

Only five percent of employers feel that education and skill requirements are increasing significantly.

Only 15 percent of employers report difficulty finding workers with the appropriate occupational skills. These shortages are generally in chronically underpaid 'women's' occupations and traditional craft trades.

We did find a skills shortage of sorts. The problem of preparing young people who are reliable, presentable and who communicate well on the job should not be taken lightly. For the people who lack them, these skills often prove permanent obstacles to acquiring meaningful employment.

But in a broad survey of employment needs across America, we found little evidence of a far-reaching desire for a more educated workforce.

Where Are People Working?

The evident absence of a serious shortage of people with strong cognitive skills is easier to understand after an examination of the places where most Americans work.

Despite the central position that a college education plays in the American dream, the United States employs one and a half times as many janitors, nearly twice as many secretaries and five times as many clerks as all the lawyers, accountants, investment bankers, stock brokers and computer programmers combined.

Despite the decline of the agricultural sector in our high-tech society, America still employs more than two million farm workers compared with 854,000 doctors and dentists. There are 1.8 million engineers in America, but 6.2 million people work as retail sales clerks and more than 18 million on factory floors.

All told, more than 70 percent of the jobs in America will not require a college education by the year 2000. These jobs are the backbone of our economy, and the productivity of workers in these jobs will make or break our economic future.

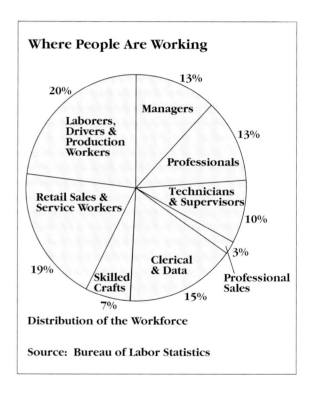

Where People Are Working

- 20% — Laborers, Drivers & Production Workers
- 13% — Managers
- 13% — Professionals
- 10% — Technicians & Supervisors
- 3% — Professional Sales
- 15% — Clerical & Data
- 7% — Skilled Crafts
- 19% — Retail Sales & Service Workers

Distribution of the Workforce

Source: Bureau of Labor Statistics

What Skills Do Jobs Require?

According to our survey of national skill requirements, as confirmed by the Bureau of Labor Statistics, jobs held by the total United States workforce can be categorized as follows:

- More than one third require little more than an eighth grade education.

- More than one third require a basic education plus some additional non-college skills.

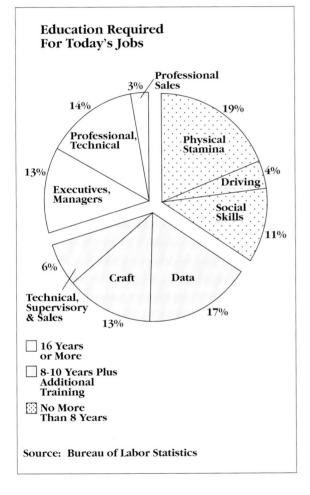

Education Required For Today's Jobs

- Professional Sales 19%
- Physical Stamina
- Driving 4%
- Social Skills 11%
- Data 17%
- Craft 13%
- Technical, Supervisory & Sales 6%
- Executives, Managers 13%
- Professional, Technical 14%
- 3%

- ☐ 16 Years or More
- ☐ 8-10 Years Plus Additional Training
- ▦ No More Than 8 Years

Source: Bureau of Labor Statistics

- Less than one third require a four-year college degree.

Category 1: Out of 117 million employed workers in 1989, 40 million, or 34 percent, were employed in jobs that required less than a high-school education. These are the people who work behind counters, clean offices, make hotel beds, drive buses, take care of the sick and elderly, grow, prepare and serve food, wash dishes and work in factories. Most of these jobs require only eighth grade level math and communication skills. A pleasant personality behind the service counter, physical stamina on the construction site or a steady hand on the wheel tend to be the important requirements.

Category 2: Forty-two million people are employed in jobs in America that require a significant amount of training beyond a basic education, but not a four-year college degree. In this group fall the traditional skilled workers — apprenticed trades, auto mechanics, secretaries and data workers, firefighters, electricians, plumbers and technicians. It was in these jobs that we found occupation-specific skills shortages most often mentioned.

Category 3: The last group of 35 million people are in jobs that are likely to require a four-year college degree. Workers in this category include managers, financial analysts, accountants, salespeople, doctors,

. . . jobs held by the total United States workforce can be categorized as follows:

- *More than one third require little more than an eighth grade education.*

- *More than one third require a basic education plus some additional non-college skills.*

- *Less than one third require a four-year college degree.*

Is There A Skills Shortage?

lawyers, teachers and engineers. These people have gained the most income as the real wages of workers in the other two categories have declined.

Is America Changing The Way It Works?

The distribution of jobs among these three categories has changed only slightly over the last 17 years. The proportion of jobs in both the unskilled and skilled craft categories has dropped only three to four percentage points each from their levels in 1972 (from 37 percent to 34 percent in the first category, 40 percent to 36 percent in the second).

The management and professional jobs of Category 3 have increased from 23 to 30 percent since 1972. Even more significant, a higher number of people occupying these jobs are now graduates of four-year colleges — close to half overall, and more than three quarters of new entrants.

The major 'skills gap' defined by the *Workforce 2000* report is simply a continuation of this trend. An increasing number of all new jobs created in Category 3 in the next decade will require a four-year college degree.

We found no other major change in skill requirements on the horizon. The introduction of new technology increases job skill requirements for some, but lowers skill requirements for others. A computer can be used both as a tool to expand the informa-

tion available to a worker, thereby increasing responsibilities, or it can be used to remove responsibility and judgment from a worker by standardizing procedures and limiting responses. The latter 'de-skills' jobs, while the former increases skill requirements. In our survey we found more examples of de-skilling.

What Is The Challenge We Face?

With some exceptions, the education and skill levels of American workers roughly match the demands of their jobs.

The vast majority of our businesses are not planning any major reorganization of the way work is done that would affect this equilibrium.

Although the demand for college graduates will probably rise over the decade, this will not dramatically alter the character of our labor market, nor create a crisis. Four-year college graduates have been increasing as a percentage of our workforce since 1940 — from six percent in that year, to 11 percent in 1959, to 22 percent in 1987. A continuation of this trend will bring us to the 30 percent that is likely to be required by the year 2000.

We will face a challenge similar to that faced by many Third World countries, to instill in our youth the attitude and social manners required for work in an advanced industrial nation. We will also have to fill selected occupational shortages that emerge. And, we will have to make provisions for day care as well as English classes for immigrant workers.

Meeting these challenges will not be easy. But if we meet them, we will no longer have a skills gap.

However, simply meeting these challenges will not raise our living standard.

By preparing more Americans for today's jobs we will, at best, perpetuate the nation's current slow rate of productivity growth and the incomes of most American workers will slide.

But there is an alternative . . .

By preparing more Americans for today's jobs we will, at best, perpetuate the nation's current slow rate of productivity growth and the incomes of most American workers will slide. But there is an alternative . . .

3

AMERICA'S WORKERS: DISPOSABLE RESOURCE OR COMPETITIVE ADVANTAGE?

The stories in this chapter are true; the names of people have been changed and one of the plants is described anonymously.

Joe Smith is a Vietnam vet who works in an electrical control panel plant in the Midwest.

For the past 15 years, Joe has been punching holes into the metal sheets that form the panel casing. Seven or eight hundred times a day he pulls the metal sheets off the conveyor belt, aligns them on the drill press, activates the drill, watches as the press comes crashing down, removes the sheets from the press, wipes away the metal flashing from around the holes and then returns the sheets to the conveyor belt.

The monotony is interrupted every so often when Joe's machine breaks down or when a problem crops up down the line and the service people come to fix it. Sometimes, too, the forklift operators deliver the wrong materials or the set-up people have to readjust the machines when the plant is running a new batch.

Joe earns about $9 per hour ($13.50 when he gets overtime) plus health insurance and pension benefits. Between his $25,000 salary and his wife's $15,000 salary from her job at the bank, his family gets along pretty well.

Lately, though, Joe has begun to worry. The company introduced a new kind of snap-on panel that looks as if it may replace the one he makes. Joe has noticed that the new job is not a career job. Most of the workers are young — practically kids — and they earn only $6 per hour. They do not receive the benefits Joe gets.

Last year, a friend of Joe's lost his job when the company moved the wire harness department to Mexico. His friend finally found a $6-per-hour job as a shopping mall security guard. Now his friend's family is having trouble paying the mortgage. At 38-years-old and with only a high-school diploma, Joe worries that if he loses his job he will not fare any better.

Sam Lopresti was assigned to manage Joe's plant two years ago because the plant was not earning much money. Sam's role was to cut costs and turn the plant around. He chose to do this by replacing well paid workers with lower paid ones through outsourcing and by product redesign to use less materials and labor. So far he has saved the company $20 million.

Our wages are five times higher than those in Taiwan and Singapore, six times higher than in South Korea and nine times higher than in Mexico. Increasingly, fierce competition has forced American companies to cut costs aggressively.

Employers are responding to this pressure in a number of ways. One way is to move production to low wage countries, closing down American plants and becoming importers. Another is to replace workers with machines. A third is to lower labor costs by cutting wages and benefits; replacing higher paid workers with lower paid ones.

Sam Lopresti was assigned to manage Joe's plant two years ago because the plant was not earning much money. Sam's role was to cut costs and turn the plant around. He chose to do this by replacing well paid workers with lower paid ones through outsourcing and by product redesign to use less materials and labor. So far he has saved the company $20 million.

For example, Sam found that by moving the wire harness assembly department to Mexico, he could replace workers he was paying $12 per hour (including benefits) with dollar-per-hour labor. Within the plant, Sam's engineers found a way to snap the panel case together. The proposal was a double winner. It eliminated the need to drill holes and bolt the panels together, saving labor. Moreover, the simple assembly allowed Sam to hire $6-per-hour temporary workers to replace the more expensive career machine operators.

"The panel is too big to move to Mexico," Sam explains. "But it really bugs me to pay $12 an hour for people to use screwdrivers. My 10-year-old son can do that."

Sam now plans to expand the practice of snapping on panels. "We'll save almost $1.5 million on that project alone," he says. "We feel the Japanese breathing down our necks in this industry; we have to cut costs or we're history."

Joe will lose his job this year.

Across our nation today, millions of workers face situations similar to Joe's. To stay competitive, many companies are increasingly trying to cut the cost of labor.

Why is this happening? There are many reasons, but one of the most serious is increased competition. Our wages are five times higher than those in Taiwan and Singapore, six times higher than in South Korea and nine times higher than in Mexico.

Increasingly, fierce competition has forced American companies to cut costs aggressively. Deregulation of service industries like transportation, banking and telecommunications has intensified domestic competition and forced cost cuts. Public employers have been forced by funding cuts to adopt stringent efficiency measures as well.

Employers are responding to this pressure in a number of ways. One way is to move production to low wage countries, closing down American plants and becoming importers. Another is to replace workers with machines. A third is to lower labor costs by cutting wages and benefits; replacing higher paid workers with lower paid ones.

American companies have adopted all three approaches. Some 700 American companies employ more than 350,000 people in Singapore, Mexico and Taiwan alone. Many more companies import products to sell under their own brand labels — goods ranging from air conditioners to microwave ovens and VCRs. Service companies, like retailers and wholesalers that cannot move offshore, are cutting the benefits of their long-term workers and increasingly resorting to part-time or temporary labor to keep wages and benefits down.

Public employers are also taking drastic steps. Some are instituting hiring freezes and reducing services. Others are using private contractors who pay lower wages to perform public services. In order to meet immediate cash needs, investments in public infrastructure are being reduced.

The employers instituting these changes are not necessarily Scrooges; they are responding to real economic pressures. They see no other way to survive.

But there is another way.

An Alternative

Six years ago, an IBM circuit board factory in Austin, Texas was in big trouble. Executives from IBM's personal computer plant complained to top management that they could buy the boards elsewhere and save the company $60 million. Why should they continue buying from Austin?

For many companies, $60 million in savings would have been enough reason to close the plant. But IBM has a full employ-ment practice that discourages closing plants and firing workers, so the company gave Austin a chance to become competitive.

Unlike Sam Lopresti at the control panel plant, the Austin managers decided to cut costs by changing work organization. The plant had huge indirect costs. For every direct worker building the circuit boards, two or three indirect workers were required to move materials, inspect quality, repair mistakes, maintain the machines, schedule and supervise. Despite the efforts of countless supervisors, planners and inspectors, too many boards were shipped with defects and costly inventory lay all around the plant.

The IBM managers tackled the problem by upgrading skills. They organized their line workers into teams, giving each group responsibility for its own inspection, repair, maintenance, material ordering and supervision. They assigned indirect workers to the teams and gave them direct production tasks. The ratio of indirect to direct workers was reduced to less than one-to-one.

The IBM executives also changed job classifications by reorganizing manufacturing slots into seven categories (manufacturing technical associates [MTA's]) based upon skill requirements. Workers' performance on competency tests determines their classification. Under the earlier organization the career track for a manufacturing worker

*But there is another way . . .
the Austin managers decided
to cut costs by changing work
organization. The plant had
huge indirect costs. For
every direct worker building
the circuit boards, two or
three indirect workers were
required to move materials,
inspect quality, repair
mistakes, maintain the
machines, schedule and
supervise . . .*

*They assigned indirect workers
to the teams and gave them
direct production tasks.*

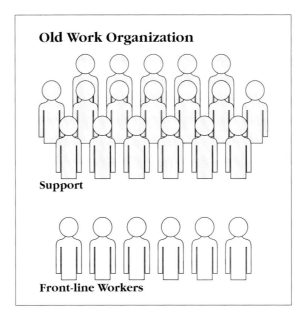

Old Work Organization

Support

Front-line Workers

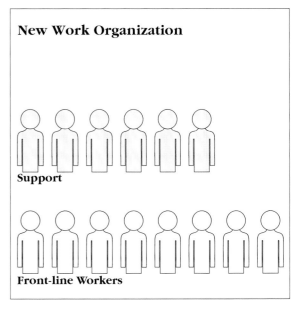

New Work Organization

Support

Front-line Workers

ended after about five years. By contrast, the new MTA system provides opportunities for advancement through the fifteenth or twentieth year, with each level requiring a higher degree of skill or responsibility.

Vera Sharbonez had worked at the Austin plant ever since she left high school in 1969. Her job was to feed circuit boards into the automatic insertion machine which rapidly fitted each board with more than 50 transistors and capacitors. When the machine had completed its work, she pulled the board out, inspected it for mistakes and put it in the 'pass' or 'reject' bin. She did this about 1,200 times a day. Her pay was $10 per hour.

When rumors started spreading about trouble at the plant five years ago, Vera worried that she might lose her job. Good jobs were scarce in Texas, and she needed the money she earned at IBM.

Instead, Vera was able to keep her job. She was assigned to a new team of production workers. The team included people from all areas of the plant. They were told that, in addition to their old tasks, they would have to learn a range of new skills. Vera would not only operate the insertion machine but also set it up at the beginning of the day and fix it when it broke down. She and the others would be responsible for setting their own schedules and they would take turns leading the team.

"When the MTA system was introduced, I was worried," Vera recalls. "I wasn't sure that I could do the new jobs. I thought that management was just trying to get more work out of us for the same pay."

To prepare Vera and her co-workers, IBM launched a major education and training initiative for its workforce, some of whom lacked a high-school education. The plant now spends more than five percent of total payroll (not including lost wages) to teach workers how to maintain machinery, plan production, troubleshoot electronic circuitry and use computers. In some cases, workers had to be taught basic reading and math before they could take the other courses.

Today, Vera's group meets to discuss the day's work plan each morning. They order their own materials from the storeroom, they speak with internal suppliers about materials problems and talk with customers about quality. The team keeps its own quality records and helps with decisions about what equipment to purchase. Vera still spends 25 percent of her time loading boards, but it is only one of the many jobs she knows how to do.

"I've been working a lot harder the past few years than before, but it's worth it. I feel like they're treating me like an adult now. I can make decisions. I am also learning things that will be useful to me in all kinds of jobs. If management would give us the production goals, I think we could run the whole plant now!"

Workers at IBM Austin also help make investment decisions. Frank Jones and his co-workers in the lamination area, for example, decided to build a better 'clean room' environment. They studied alternate systems, worked with potential vendors, conducted a cost/benefit analysis and helped design and order the equipment.

Improvements have made the Austin plant competitive with its rivals. The $60 million gap has been closed. Productivity has improved by more than 200 percent and quality by five times, and inventory has been reduced by 40 percent. Despite the improved productivity, no one has been laid off at the plant (though IBM does have an early retirement plan). As the plant has become more competitive, production has expanded by 600 percent, a new product is being introduced and the facility is employing more people than ever before. Management plans to extend the new organization much further, delegating even broader responsibilities to the line workers.

Which Choice?

The managers at IBM Austin and at the control panel plant were both trying to cut costs to be more competitive. But the choices they made were fundamentally different. While the panel plant achieved 75 percent of its cost improvements by paying

To prepare Vera and her co-workers, IBM launched a major education and training initiative for its workforce, some of whom lacked a high-school education. The plant now spends more than five percent of total payroll (not including lost wages) to teach workers how to maintain machinery, plan production, troubleshoot electronic circuitry and use computers.

The managers at IBM Austin and at the control panel plant were both trying to cut costs to be more competitive. But the choices they made were fundamentally different. While the panel plant achieved 75 percent of its cost improvements by paying lower wages, IBM Austin achieved more than 90 percent of its improvement through greater productivity with no net loss in employment.

lower wages, IBM Austin achieved more than 90 percent of its improvement through greater productivity with no net loss in employment.

Why didn't Sam Lopresti try a skills upgrade approach? For him, the choice seemed too risky. "It would take too much investment to try to educate the guys we have here to take more responsibility," he said. "Many aren't even high-school graduates. I've read about these factories that are giving power to the workers and expecting them to act like college grads. That's academic stuff. It sounds great in the classroom, but it would take years even if you could make it work, which I doubt. I don't have years to turn this place around."

The IBM managers, though dealing with a similarly educated workforce, did not have Sam Lopresti's option; the company's full employment practice discourages layoffs. As IBM's managers note, good quality is hard to get with a low wage, high turnover philosophy.

From a management point of view, both approaches worked. Both turned around unprofitable plants. In the short run, either choice was a good one. For the nation, however, the choice has serious long-term implications. High productivity work organizations mean the jobs stay at home. Job security increases, as do wages.

4

THE ORGANIZATION OF WORK IN AMERICA

The organization of America's workplaces today is largely modeled after the manufacturing system made famous by Henry Ford in the early 20th century. Frederick Winslow Taylor conceived the system to provide an efficient way to organize mass production with a large population of low skilled workers. The premise is simple: Break complex jobs down into a myriad of simple rote tasks, which the worker then repeats with machine-like efficiency. The system was designed on the correct assumption for the early 1900's that educated workers would be hard to find.

The system is managed by a small group of educated planners and supervisors who do the thinking for the organization, plan strategy, implement changes, motivate workers and solve problems. An extensive, hierarchical supervisory structure and elaborate administrative procedures allow managers to keep control of a large number of workers.

Most employees under the Taylor model need not be educated. It is far more important that they be reliable, steady and willing to follow directions. The managers do the thinking, technology furnishes the productivity advances and the operators simply supply grease for the wheel.

The America of the 1950's and 1960's prospered with the Taylor model. Immigrants arriving at our shores and farmers migrating to the cities furnished a limitless supply of low skilled labor. America's vast domestic market also encouraged capital investment for mass production. The United States embraced the system more firmly than any other country.

This system helped make our nation rich and, in earlier decades, made the United States the largest manufacturer with the largest middle class of any country in the world. The system still determines the way we organize our schools, our offices, our banks and our hospitals. And it continues to define the job expectations of workers like Joe and Vera, as well as the options that managers like Sam are willing to consider.

Most employees under the Taylor model need not be educated. It is far more important that they be reliable, steady and willing to follow directions. The managers do the thinking, technology furnishes the productivity advances . . .

As a new century approaches, however, this old work organization is becoming less appropriate for a high wage nation. High speed communication and transportation make it possible to produce most products and services anywhere in the world. Modern machinery and production methods can therefore be combined with low wage workers to drive costs down.

Why Mass Production Is Outdated

As a new century approaches, however, this old work organization is becoming less appropriate for a high wage nation. High speed communication and transportation make it possible to produce most products and services anywhere in the world. Modern machinery and production methods can therefore be combined with low wage workers to drive costs down.

High wage nations like the United States can succeed only by producing higher quality products, providing customers with greater product variety, introducing new products more frequently and creating automated systems which are more complex than those that can be operated in low wage countries.

These requirements increase production complexity, making it difficult for a small group of managers at the center to control their businesses through administrative procedures.

Under the Taylor system, more planners are needed to develop procedures for new product introductions; more schedulers are needed to schedule greater product variety; more set-up and maintenance people are needed to handle the automated systems; and more checkers are needed to check the checkers already in place to ensure high quality.

Surrounding the direct-line worker doing his or her two minute job in a factory, for example, is an army of indirect support workers setting up and maintaining machines; inspecting and reworking faulty products; receiving, storing and delivering materials to the line; cleaning up; running the utilities; producing computer runs of parts, orders, schedules and performance; hiring and firing employees; designing products and processes and assuring quality. In addition, several layers of managers exist to supervise all of this.

Mass production has become highly bureaucratic and less efficient than it was. An increasing number of production steps and indirect processes means more hand-offs of information, parts and finished products. This, plus the growing number of dependencies, lengthens production time and causes a dramatic increase in mistakes.

In back offices of 'Tayloristic' insurance companies, for example, forms are passed from one worker to another in assembly line fashion. Functionaries take longer to process forms, make mistakes that must be corrected and shuffle customers who have made telephone inquiries from department to department. Each specialized worker knows only a single part of the form and has no authority to solve a customer problem that goes beyond a narrowly defined area.

As policy options increase, new forms of risk are insured and computers are increasingly used to store and process information, work becomes more complex and change becomes a way of life. The number of tasks to be performed increases exponentially, and the tasks change often. To control all of this, administrative guidelines, work procedures and indirect functions multiply until bureaucracy overwhelms efficiency and quality.

An Alternative: High Performance Work Organizations

Managers, however, do have another choice. Across the United States and throughout high wage countries around the world, some companies have been adopting a completely new style of work. The guiding principle of this new work organization is to reduce bureaucracy by giving authority to direct workers for a wider variety of tasks.

Workers are asked to use judgment and make decisions rather than follow, by rote, cumbersome procedures spelled out in detail. Management layers disappear as front-line workers take over many of the tasks that others used to do — from quality control to production scheduling. Tasks formerly performed by dozens of unskilled individuals are now performed by fewer highly skilled people.

New forms of work organization apply in some form to almost every industry. In a traditional American bank, for example, the functions of a teller are usually limited to accepting deposits, cashing checks and recording loan and bill payments. The position is highly specialized. Some tellers deal with commercial clients, others with foreign currency transactions, others with travelers' cheques and still others with small account customers.

If a customer has a more complex transaction, seeks financial advice or is interested in bank 'products,' the teller refers the customer to a back-up department, staffed in large part by college-educated customer service representatives. Some banks have even instituted different groups of back-up personnel who are organized by the complexity of the customer issue. The entire 'front office' system — from automatic teller machines to tellers, from customer service and sales representatives to loan officers — is organized by operations managers to move customers in and out of the bank as quickly as possible. It is a highly 'Tayloristic' work design.

Most American banks have a turnover rate among tellers that averages more than 40 percent a year, and in some branches can approach 200 percent. Salaries are low, starting at about $14,000 annually. Pressure is high to perform one's duties accurately and quickly, and advancement is limited. Training for these jobs consists of four to six weeks of orientation and practice.

In a number of European banks, such as Hypo, Dresdner and the Bavarian Bank in Germany, work is now being reorganized to

The guiding principle of this new work organization is to reduce bureaucracy by giving authority to direct workers for a wider variety of tasks . . . Management layers disappear as front-line workers take over many of the tasks that others used to do.

New forms of work organization apply in some form to almost every industry.

In a number of European banks ... work is now being reorganized to assign greater responsibility to skilled financial 'clerks'. ... They handle all the functions of the average American teller, plus open new accounts, grant mortgages and loans, process commercial, foreign and consumer transactions, provide investment advice and sell stocks and bonds — functions performed by specialized departments in traditional American banks.

assign greater responsibility to skilled financial 'clerks.' The individuals who fill these positions are actually viewed as 'front office' professionals, rather than as tellers. They handle all the functions of the average American teller, plus open new accounts, grant mortgages and loans, process commercial, foreign and consumer transactions, provide investment advice and sell stocks and bonds — functions performed by specialized departments in traditional American banks.

In some foreign banks, these workers are assigned their own clients with whom they build professional relationships. There is an emphasis on job rotation, working in small groups with other bank professionals and demonstrating some degree of competency in every banking function — both in the 'front' and 'back' offices.

The financial clerk position is regarded as an official profession for which one must train for three years in a competitive and rigorous apprenticeship program beginning at age 16. Learning does not end with the apprenticeship: a university track or an industry supported professional banking academy provides considerable opportunities for advancement.

The education foundation and the apprenticeship program that prepare young people for these professions have been in existence for decades; now in the face of increasing global competition in financial

markets, these foreign banks are redesigning work to take greater advantage of the capabilities of these well-trained employees. To be sure, not every foreign bank is making such changes; but the tools, the potential and the trend is evident.

Work reorganizations like this require big investments in training. Workers' pay levels often rise to reflect their greater qualifications and responsibilities. But the productivity and quality gains more than offset the costs to the company of higher wages and skills development.

Despite these advantages, most American companies still cling to old forms of work organization. For more than 95 percent of the companies in our survey, the control panel plant's solution is still the preferred route.

Why Companies Continue To Make The Low Wage Choice

Faced as they are with mounting foreign and domestic competitive pressures, why do most American companies stick with traditional forms of work organization? For many companies, the costs seem too high and the benefits still uncertain:

- A substantial initial investment is necessary to shift to a high productivity path. Workers and managers must be retrained. Unlike capital investment, which is an employer's to keep, companies risk losing their training investment if employees seek work elsewhere.

- Returns on investment from reorganization may take several years to realize. The perverse short-term financial horizons by which most American companies operate present tremendous obstacles to this type of investment.

- The flow of work and responsibilities must be redesigned. The transition can disrupt work processes.

- Public policy often encourages the low wage path. Our lack of national commitment to full employment makes it easier for companies to hire temporary or seasonal workers and lay them off with little consequence. Our foreign tax credit and deferral and foreign trade zone legislation provide incentives for low wage production offshore. Our equal pay law does not apply to part-time and temporary employees, making it cheaper for employers to replace full-time permanent workers with contingent workers.

American companies that overcome all the obstacles and decide to pursue high productivity work organizations run into one final obstacle that their foreign counterparts do not have to face: a front-line workforce that often needs remedial education.

As one financial services manager said to our study team, "We can pay to give remedial education to our current workers, but we can't afford to regive high-school educations to all our new hires who are high-school graduates because they didn't learn much the first time."

Or as another financial services human resources director said, "I can do my back office functions anywhere in the world now. If I can't get enough skilled workers here, I'll move the skilled jobs out of the country and just do the customer interface here."

Why Work Organization Is Pivotal

The changes taking place in work organization are key to productivity and quality improvement, the touchstones of economic success.

Steam and electricity drove the first two industrial revolutions, causing profound changes in work organization which increased productivity, quality and living standards dramatically. The creation of the factory in the 1800's and mass production in the 1900's followed these technology breakthroughs.

The advent of the computer, high speed communications and universal education are heralding a third industrial revolution. High performance work organizations are already unleashing new advances in productivity. A greater variety of high quality products and services are possible with shorter lead times between new product generations and between the placing of an order and the receipt of the product.

High performance work organizations are already unleashing new advances in productivity. A greater variety of high quality products and services are possible with shorter lead times between new product generations and between the placing of an order and the receipt of the product.

Work organization changes drive the demand for high skills. But without a skilled workforce, most companies will settle into low wage work organizations.

America implemented the mass production revolution faster than other nations, even though others — the British and Germans primarily — had pioneered more of the enabling technologies. The enabling technologies for today's new revolution have been pioneered mainly in the United States, but this does not guarantee that we will reap the greatest economic benefits. To do so, we must also lead the world toward new high performance work organizations.

Work organization changes drive the demand for high skills. But without a skilled workforce, most companies will settle into low wage work organizations.

As we shall now see, we are not now providing the education and skills to a majority of our students and workers which will be required to support a move to new high performance work organizations.

5

HOW WE PREPARE OUR CHILDREN FOR WORK

No nation has produced a highly qualified technical workforce without first providing its workers with a strong general education. America invests little in its front-line workforce. We do not expect much from them in school. We give them few job skills and little training. And we let them sink or swim when they try to get into the workforce. Yet, these are the very people we must count on to lead the way to a competitive and productive economy.

The educational performance of those students who become front-line workers in this country is well below the average performance of their counterparts in some newly industrializing low wage countries. Our front-line workers will not be able to compete in the economic arena because they are increasingly unable to compete in the educational arena. They are fast becoming unemployable at American wage levels.

In our expectations for young people, the resources that we devote to them and the rewards for performance that we give them, our whole system conspires to produce minimal educational effort or achievement among our students who are not college bound.

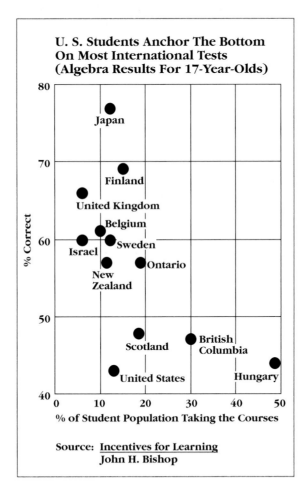

U. S. Students Anchor The Bottom On Most International Tests (Algebra Results For 17-Year-Olds)

% Correct

% of Student Population Taking the Courses

Source: <u>Incentives for Learning</u>
John H. Bishop

America invests little in its front-line workforce. We do not expect much from them in school. We give them few job skills and little training. And we let them sink or swim when they try to get into the workforce.

Our front-line workers will not be able to compete in the economic arena because they are increasingly unable to compete in the educational arena. They are fast becoming unemployable at American wage levels.

Our educational system is almost wholly oriented toward the needs of the college bound. We provide very little for the majority of this nation's youth who do not go to four-year colleges.

One in five American children grows up in Third World surroundings . . . many of these children start out with severe learning disadvantages from which they never recover.

Two Tracks From The Starting Line

Beginning in elementary school, students are sorted and grouped within their classrooms by ability. In the early grades, these groups are often given birds' names, like 'Bluebirds' and 'Robins.'

Louis, a 'Bluebird' in a third grade class, spends the reading hour sounding out words on a blackboard one by one. His teacher 'knows' that his ability is low, so she doesn't push him hard.

Jim, a 'Robin' in Louis' class, sits by himself at a desk on the other side of the room. He and the rest of the 'Robins' are expected to read a certain number of stories per week and write mini-reports on their favorite story.

Seven years later, Louis and Jim no longer go to the same classes:

In his general math class, Louis is learning to calculate sales tax on a grocery bill. For his homework assignment, he is supposed to add columns of figures together and then apply percentages to the total.

Down the hall, Jim has been working on problems in analytical geometry for the past hour. Next period, he and his lab partners will work on the design of a simple software program to control a toy robot they are building.

Louis represents nearly half of all high-school students, those who are relegated to 'general curriculum' courses to learn 'life survival skills.' It is a path to nowhere for Louis and the others who go on to become America's front-line workers.

Jim, on the other hand, will go on to college. There, he will be given the skills, knowledge and credentials he needs to direct the front-line workers of this nation.

Students who enter the workforce rather than attend college or post-secondary vocational-technical training, account for only about 25 percent of all secondary school vocational credits. Surprisingly, students headed for college account for nearly 48 percent of these vocational credits. Less than one eighth of general education students enter a job with any occupation-specific vocational education preparation. As a result, the 'general curriculum' ends up providing neither strong academic skills nor strong vocational skills.

Our educational system is almost wholly oriented toward the needs of the college bound. We provide very little for the majority of this nation's youth who do not go to four-year colleges. The story starts early, in the conditions under which many of our front-line workers grow up, and the resources that we provide them while in school.

Special Problems Of The Poor

One in five American children grows up in Third World surroundings. Often living in communities where they are surrounded by hunger, violence and drug addiction, many of these children start out with severe learning disadvantages from which they never recover.

Poor children pose a significant challenge to educators, and their special problems often require extra attention. Schools by themselves cannot be expected to bring these children up to world class standards. Their job is made even more difficult, if not impossible, by the financing of the system.

Since almost half of the funding for public education is drawn from local property taxes, the financial system favors those who are most likely to go to college — the children of the economically advantaged. (In Ohio, for example, poor communities spend as little as $2,500 per pupil while wealthier areas spend up to $10,000.)

Affluent school districts also benefit disproportionately from state educational funding. State aid is generally based on pupil attendance. Because dropout rates are lower in wealthier areas, they end up with more money for their secondary school age students than do poor districts. Schools with the largest percentage of disadvantaged students offer 40 percent fewer vocational courses and facilities, one third as many occupational programs, and one half as many advanced courses as schools with the smallest percentage of disadvantaged students.

This nation cannot hope to produce a world class workforce without addressing these problems.

Expectations And Standards

As a society, we do not seem to expect much of the students who are not headed for college.

In fact, the difference between Louis and Jim lies mainly in the expectations that the adults in their lives have for them. From an early age, the adults in Louis' life told him that he had little academic ability. Believing it, he did not display any. But everyone expected much of Jim, and he performed. More than any other country in the world, the United States believes that natural ability, rather than effort, explains achievement.

The tragedy is that we communicate to millions of students every year, especially to low income and minority students, that we do not believe they have what it takes to learn. They then live up to our expectations, despite evidence that they can meet very high performance standards under the right conditions.

Most employers look at the high-school diploma as evidence of staying power, not of academic achievement. The vast majority of them do not even ask to see a transcript. They realized long ago that it is possible to graduate from high school in this country and still be functionally illiterate.

As a result, despite recent attempts to tighten up graduation requirements in many states, the non-college bound know that their performance in high school is likely to have little or no bearing on the type of employment they manage to find.

... we communicate to millions of students every year, especially to low income and minority students, that we do not believe they have what it takes to learn. They then live up to our expectations ...

... the non-college bound know that their performance in high school is likely to have little or no bearing on the type of employment they manage to find.

The Transition From School To Work

Although the vast majority of our young people leave high school to go directly to work, we typically offer them little or no assistance in this transition.

Few large firms in the United States will employ students who have just graduated from high school, preferring to wait until they have established some sort of track record elsewhere. Family and friends can often help middle class youngsters gain their first chance in the workplace. But poor and minority students in the inner cities and impoverished rural areas rarely have such help. Certain they will be rejected out-of-hand by middle class employers who will not like the way they talk, dress and behave, many give up early, both on school and work.

The result is that typical high-school graduates mill about in the labor market, moving from one dead-end job to another until the age of 23 or 24. Then, with little more in the way of skills than they had at 18, they move into the regular labor market, no match for the highly trained German, Danish, Swedish or Swiss youth of 19.

Most secondary schools provide little opportunity for the student to build a bridge to the workplace and gain, while in school, the values, habits and skills that European youth naturally acquire through their training and mentoring during apprenticeship programs. (In America, the apprenticeship system is not designed or perceived as a school-to-work transition program — the average apprentice in the United States is older than age 29.)

Some vocational educators are moving to put more academic substance into their offerings. Some are creating technology curricula that incorporate demanding mathematics and science studies in an approach that enables students to apply what they are learning to challenging technological problems. Some 1,500 students are enrolled in school-to-apprenticeship programs based on the European model.

Some high schools are pairing up with community colleges to offer combined programs that promise a real future to their vocational graduates. Some business organizations have worked with school districts to initiate high-school academies that offer good connections to technical careers in business. And some elite vocational schools have always done a good job of preparing their students for good careers. But these programs, promising as they are, hardly constitute a system.

The fact remains that our secondary schools are not organized to meet the needs of employers or work-bound students. Even the vocational education system does a better job of placing its students in post-secondary educational institutions than placing them in jobs related to their course of study. The guidance system is set up to

. . . typical high-school graduates mill about in the labor market, moving from one dead-end job to another until the age of 23 or 24. Then, with little more in the way of skills than they had at 18, they move into the regular labor market, no match for the highly trained German, Danish, Swedish or Swiss youth of 19.

help students get into college. Employers who ask for transcripts typically find them very difficult to obtain, but colleges are able to receive them easily. There is no curriculum to meet the needs of non-college bound youth, no real employment service for those who go right to work, few guidance services for them, no certification of their accomplishment and, as we have mentioned, no rewards in the workplace for hard work in school.

Dropouts

Currently, more than 20 percent of our nation's students drop out before completing high school (the figure is as high as 50 percent in many inner cities). Not only do we make little effort to help our potential dropouts in school, but once they do drop out, our society makes even less of an effort to recover them. Some dropouts do come back at their own initiative and expense to earn their school equivalency certificates, but only after many years wasted in unproductive employment.

Ironically, schools and governments reap substantial short-term benefits when a student drops out. For example, the average annual per pupil expenditure for a student in school is approximately $4,300. When a student drops out, the school's costs drop.

By comparison, overall spending in employment and training programs for dropouts is relatively low. While some programs have per participant costs equal to or greater than the per pupil expenditures in schools, only a small fraction of the eligible population is enrolled in these 'second chance' programs. If the total federal, state and local funding for 'second chance' programs were applied to all current dropouts, we would spend the equivalent of only $235 annually per dropout in the nation.

This perverse incentive system essentially allows us to balance our education budgets on the backs of our school dropouts.

Over the long run, however, we pay. Our welfare and unemployment systems, our prisons, and, ultimately, the national economy are continually drained by the cost of sustaining an uneducated, unproductive individual in our society.

The Finish Line

We expect very little academic accomplishment from the students who are not in the academic college bound curriculum; we give them watered down courses and we provide them with very few opportunities for participating in effective applied learning programs or for acquiring relevant, professional-level qualifications for occupations.

- We have no national system capable of setting high academic standards for the non-college bound or of assessing their achievement against those standards.

There is no curriculum to meet the needs of non-college bound youth, no real employment service for those who go right to work, few guidance services for them, no certification of their accomplishment and, as we have mentioned, no rewards in the workplace for hard work in school.

Not only do we make little effort to help our potential dropouts in school, but once they do drop out, our society makes even less of an effort to recover them.

This perverse incentive system essentially allows us to balance our education budgets on the backs of our school dropouts.

Our future depends on having highly skilled, highly motivated workers on the front line. That is not what our education system was designed to produce.

- We make very little provision for facilitating the school-to-work transition. It is especially difficult for students who know few adults to help them gain their first job or acquire the habits, attitudes and values that will enable them to keep that job once they get it. High-school guidance offices focus their efforts on the students going off to college, not on those bound for work.

- We do almost nothing to recover our students who drop out of school — almost one quarter of all our students — one third of whom will go on to become our front-line workforce.

- We provide far more financial support for districts with high proportions of students who usually attend four-year colleges than we do for districts serving our future front-line workforce.

America will not be able to choose a high productivity, high wage future unless it charts a sharp change of course. Our future depends on having highly skilled, highly motivated workers on the front line. That is not what our education system was designed to produce.

6

THE EDUCATION AND TRAINING OF AMERICA'S ADULT WORKERS

Each year, American employers spend an estimated $30 billion on formal training. At most, however, only one third of this amount is spent on our non-college edu-cated workforce, affecting no more than eight percent of our front-line workers. The occasional training which companies do provide for these workers is generally limited to orientation training for new hires or 'team building' and motivational training for long-term employees. The one exception is the ongoing training provided for skilled crafts-people.

Only a small fraction of firms make a significant investment in training workers. According to the American Society for Training and Development, $27 billion of that $30 billion was paid out by 15,000 employers (one half of one percent of all American employers). And, of this small universe of firms that actually train, only 100 to 200 — the largest companies with signifi-cant professional and managerial staff — spend more than two percent of their payroll on formal training.

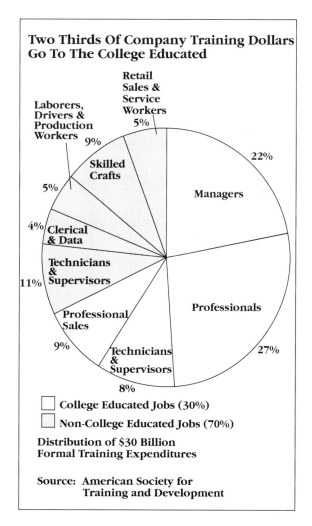

Two Thirds Of Company Training Dollars Go To The College Educated

Retail Sales & Service Workers 5%

Laborers, Drivers & Production Workers 9%

Skilled Crafts 5%

Clerical & Data 4%

Technicians & Supervisors 11%

Professional Sales 9%

Technicians & Supervisors 8%

Managers 22%

Professionals 27%

☐ College Educated Jobs (30%)
▨ Non-College Educated Jobs (70%)

Distribution of $30 Billion Formal Training Expenditures

Source: American Society for Training and Development

Each year, American employers spend an estimated $30 billion on formal training . . .$27 billion of that $30 billion was paid out by 15,000 employers (one half of one percent of all American employers).

The $30 billion spent by companies on training represents less than 10 percent of the nation's annual public education budget. We thus devote almost all of our educational resources to the first 15 to 20 years of life. We assume that little learning will be required during the subsequent 40 to 50 years of working life, especially for front-line workers.

Apprentices are part of the small minority of front-line workers who benefit from extensive, long-term training. These are skilled workers — construction tradespeople, operating engineers and tool and die makers.

The apprenticeship system usually combines paid work with classroom and workplace instruction. Training is systematic. Clear industry established standards and regular performance assessments lead to nationally recognized certification.

National industry based networks of unions and employers often help design the curricula and provide the locally administered programs with an infrastructure of support. Federal and state education funds support buildings and the cost of instructors.

Apprenticeship programs sponsored by unions and companies provide coherent training to develop the skills of adult workers. Though worthwhile programs, they serve less than 300,000 people at any given time — less than three tenths of one percent of our workforce.

We thus devote almost all of our educational resources to the first 15 to 20 years of life. We assume that little learning will be required during the subsequent 40 to 50 years of working life, especially for front-line workers.

The fact that employers in this country do not spend much money on training of front-line workers is not surprising. The 'Taylor' model of work organization still followed by most of our companies does not require skills from the vast majority of their workers.

Americans have traditionally relied on the marketplace to determine how much educational preparation is necessary for work. We assume that companies will train their workers if it makes business sense, and that individuals will seek training if they feel it will improve their career prospects. However, most employers require little in the way of skills for most workers, so market demand for training is weak. And, information — critical to efficient market functioning — about the quality of training programs is largely unavailable. The result is relatively little training for the average worker.

Foundations For Public Labor Market Policy

Modern public labor market policy in America has its origins in the Great Depression. The Federal and state governments created the Unemployment Insurance system (UI) to provide temporary economic assistance to laid off workers. To help these workers, a national network of local offices was developed through a state administered employment service system.

To protect workers, the government established minimum wage laws, pension and insurance benefits standards, health and safety laws and child labor guidelines. Federal ground rules for labor and management relations were also set. The employment service network was originally used by the Federal government to link income maintenance, job search and training together, but that assignment has eroded over time.

While skills development has never been a central focus of American labor market policy, a whole series of programs has grown on the periphery. Education, social and economic development policy initiatives have come to incorporate training as part of their missions. What we are left with is a complex and fragmented network of adult training efforts.

Education Initiatives

Though they were not designed to do so, state supported community colleges and federal Pell Grants and Guaranteed Student Loans have had a major impact on adult vocational training. More and more, public and proprietary educational institutions are becoming contract training providers to private employers and to public agencies.

In 1947, the Truman report identified the need for a community college system. Originally conceived as 'stepping stones' to four-year colleges, community colleges are now used primarily by recent high-school

graduates and adults for vocationally related training. Today, over 1,200 community colleges annually serve five million people in degree programs and another 4.5 million in non-credit courses, and they consume $12 billion in state funds. More than two thirds of the classes they provide today are for adult vocational education.

For adults who seek to upgrade their skills, the accessibility and flexible scheduling policies of community colleges make these institutions appealing. These characteristics also encourage sporadic course taking rather than the pursuit of degrees, however, and dropout rates are high.

In addition, the lack of standards sometimes makes it difficult for students to transfer courses to other institutions or for employers to recognize the value of qualifications.

According to the National Assessment of Vocational Education, only 19 percent of a group of recent high-school graduates who entered post-secondary education completed a bachelor's (11.2 percent) or an associate's (5.9 percent) degree or a certificate (1.9 percent) within four years. The assessment highlighted the need "to help students choose a field of study, construct a coherent sequence of courses in that field, complete the course or program and find a related job."

While skills development has never been a central focus of American labor market policy, a whole series of programs has grown on the periphery. Education, social and economic development policy initiatives have come to incorporate training as part of their missions. What we are left with is a complex and fragmented network of adult training efforts.

Pell Grants and Guaranteed Student Loan programs were introduced to give poor and working class children the means to attend college. These programs helped to create a major industry of private proprietary schools, while at the same time fueling the community college system. Over 85 percent of students attending proprietary schools are funded by this public money.

For employers, community colleges and proprietary schools are natural training providers. With large teaching staffs and extensive course material, these institutions can tailor programs to a client's needs. For the institutions themselves, the extra money that comes in the form of tuition and fees make this an attractive pursuit.

Social Policy

Just as education policy has spawned a vast network of training institutions for workers, our social policies have also created a series of programs to train poor people. Lyndon Johnson's War on Poverty created a variety of targeted programs that eventually focused almost all of the Federal government's attention on short-term training programs for the economically disadvantaged. Several name changes have occurred since the 1960's, but not the type of training. Eventually, the Job Training Partnership Act (JTPA) became the umbrella.

Today, the Federal government spends roughly $5.7 billion annually on 13 major employment and training programs, two thirds of which is allocated to the JTPA.

JTPA has four major components — training assistance for economically disadvantaged youth and adults (Title IIA), the Summer Youth Employment and Training Program (Title IIB), the Job Corps and the dislocated worker programs (Title III). Each JTPA program has specific eligibility requirements, but individuals can qualify for more than one program.

Other JTPA programs provide employment and training assistance for dislocated workers, and for other target groups such as Indians, Native Alaskans, Hawaiians and migrant and seasonal workers.

While JTPA is the largest, several other federal training programs exist. Each targets a special 'needs' population. Among these populations are senior citizens, refugees and those on welfare or needing vocational rehabilitation or food stamp assistance.

A number of states have created social programs for the economically disadvantaged to supplement federal efforts.

The federal and state training programs for dislocated and disadvantaged workers are well-intentioned, and some of them do an extraordinary job. However, because the programs are designed exclusively to aid the disadvantaged and dislocated populations, benefits are marginal in the labor market and participants are stigmatized.

Due to limited funds, and their dispersion among such a large number of constituencies, these programs reach only a small portion of poor people in the country and provide only limited training assistance.

Economic Development Initiatives

Most states have created a variety of programs to attract industry. They provide low cost construction financing, subsidized land, infrastructural subsidies and a variety of services to entice firms to locate in their state.

Assistance with finding good job applicants and giving them training to make them job-ready has now become part of the service package offered by most states to companies they are seeking to attract. North Carolina was the first, in 1957, using state public education facilities, to provide 'customized training' tailored to meet the needs of new companies coming into the state. Other Southern states adopted the idea as a way to convince companies in the North that the Southern labor supply, though not industrially experienced, could be brought up to a high standard. These programs proliferated throughout the country.

In the late 1970's, firms that were already established in particular states began to complain that most new jobs resulted from expansion of existing firms, not from the arrival of new companies. They asked

state governments to spend more time and money on them, rather than 'chasing smokestacks' in other states. This led to an extension of many state training programs for growing local companies.

States added retention of firms to the list of economic development efforts during the recession of the 1980's — a time when few companies were expanding. Companies in some states became eligible for training funds to upgrade skills so that they would remain in a state.

States now spend almost $1 billion a year to train workers for new jobs and to upgrade the skills of those already in the workforce. The training is usually of short duration, though in some cases it helps companies significantly upgrade skills of selected groups of line workers. Some of these state programs also help fill specific skill shortages, such as data processing.

The Current Adult Training and Employment 'System'

The network of public training activities in the country has thus been created as a result of unrelated educational, social and economic development goals rather than from any overall vision of human resource development. These various and often unintended origins of our adult training and employment 'system' have created a bewildering array of services, programs and providers.

The network of public training activities in the country has thus been created as a result of unrelated educational, social and economic development goals rather than from any overall vision of human resource development. These various and often unintended origins of our adult training and employment 'system' have created a bewildering array of services, programs and providers.

In Michigan, for example, $800 million in combined annual state and federal funds are scattered across 70 separate training and education funding programs, administered by nine different departments of state government, and offered by innumerable local providers. In New York, 19 different units of state government distribute $725 million in job training services through more than 85 different programs. At the local labor market level, where people seek training and employers seek workers, the picture is blurred. Lack of information on provision, price and quality continually frustrates the efforts of employers, agency officials and customers to navigate the system.

Employers, government agencies and post-secondary institutions use skills classifications to plan and manage their human resource programs. But trying to define the skill content of jobs is often an impossible task. The maze of classification systems attests to this:

- Seven different classification systems are used by various federal agencies and three others by the armed services. The United States Department of Labor's *Dictionary of Occupational Titles*, one of these systems, lists some 12,000 classifications.

- More than 500 national and regional private groups set standards for selected jobs.

- The United States Department of Labor's apprenticeship program alone utilizes 97 separate industry committees to set standards for some 384 occupations.

The result is a crazy quilt of competing and overlapping policies and programs, with no coherent system of standardization or information exchange services on which various providers and agencies can rely.

How has the system become so complex? A recent Michigan task force report described the evolution of the confusion over the 30 years of government activity in employment and training as follows:

"Most new programs . . . are brought forth with little attention paid to their predecessors. Often the legislation creating programs imposes specific definitions, rules and administrative procedures for expenditures; only rarely are these dovetailed with existing programs. The end result is often policy incoherence, administrative confusion and service delivery fragmentation."

The product of this ad hoc approach to training policy development is the creation of a maze of subsystems that are often incomprehensible to those who seek to use them at a local labor market level.

Reform Efforts

There have been reform efforts over the past decade, but the reform agenda is almost as fragmented as the current adult training efforts themselves. Initiatives over the last decade include:

- Increased private sector involvement through Private Industry Councils. Business leaders, elected officials and community and education leaders share responsibility for managing programs for the disadvantaged. However, because of limited funding, these programs reach only a fraction of those eligible.

- Greater emphasis on basic skills for welfare clients. Although well-intentioned, these federal and state programs aimed at skills upgrading stress job placement rather than learning gain. As a result, participants often receive brief training and may only be eligible for low skill, low paying jobs.

- Setting performance standards. Some states have called for common performance standards and a central oversight board to collect client and labor market information, monitor performance and influence funding.

- Greater use of outcome measures. To ensure accountability, some states are beginning to use outcome measures rather than procedural requirements. Instead of job placements or graduation rates, demonstrated competencies are the benchmark.

These ongoing reform efforts have been hampered by a lack of common skills classifications that makes it nearly impossible to compare programs. Lack of agreement on how to define levels of skill mastery makes it very difficult to establish workable outcome standards. In addition, most efforts have been narrowly focused on transitional training programs for the disadvantaged rather than on building a single comprehensible system to meet the training needs of employers as well. The public and private collaboration necessary to make the market for training operate effectively for all non-college people has been largely ignored. In particular, the Job Service, at the heart of the information exchange and job-and-training connection in other nations, has been allowed to atrophy in many American communities.

Summary: The Current Situation

Post-secondary training and education for the United States workforce appears to be a collection of bureaucratic subsystems rather than an effective system addressing needs of employees and employers at the community level.

Most of America's public training programs were intended to meet a series of narrowly defined needs that were often unrelated to one another. They were never intended to constitute a coherent, unified skill development system for America's front-

No effective system exists at the local level for matching employer needs with readily available skill development programs.

line workers. No effective system exists at the local level for matching employer needs with readily available skill development programs. The lack of standardization across the system makes it difficult for workers to combine courses in a logical sequence of advancement toward higher skilled work.

Most workers receive no education or training beyond high school. The vast majority who do receive training take occasional courses that are not tied to any industry standards because such standards do not exist in the United States. Others receive some training because they are economically disadvantaged or have been dislocated from jobs. This training is usually of short duration and touches only a small number of those who need it.

A New Improved System For The Future

After the turn of the century, when the second industrial revolution spawned the mass production system, American industry pressured Congress to enact the Smith-Hughes Act, which created the American system for vocational education. This system prepared American students to work with the new machinery and in the new work systems being created. It worked well for many over time, but it has not been able to keep pace with the more rapid changes in the work place of today.

If this Commission is right, we are embarking on a third industrial revolution. This revolution will usher in new high performance work organizations that have higher skill requirements than exist today.

Our current adult training policies are ill-equipped to meet this challenge. A comprehensive employment and training policy will be required to do for this revolution in work organization what the Vocational Education Act aimed to do for the last revolution.

The change to high performance work organization, and thus the increase in the demand for skilled workers, is largely in the hands of employers who must decide which route to take.

The increased supply of skilled workers and an effective market for training will require new institutions and public-private sharing of responsibility. As we shall see in the next chapter, our major competitors already have such systems in place.

The lack of standardization across the system makes it difficult for workers to combine courses in a logical sequence of advancement toward higher skilled work.

7

VOICES FROM ABROAD

In Japan, we value all of our workers. We pay our assembly worker the same as our engineer, and we provide him with the same amount of training. America is now more a country of economic hierarchy than Japan.

Japanese plant manager

America is not the only nation trying to maintain high living standards while competing with low wage nations. Germany, Japan, Sweden, Denmark and other advanced industrial countries with high wage rates face the same challenge. Here, however, the similarity stops. While America has had a negative trade balance of more than $100 billion annually for the past six years, Germany and Japan have enjoyed highly positive balances. Sweden's and Denmark's trade balances have been about even.

Each of these nations has maintained higher rates of productivity growth than the United States, and their living standards and real wages have been rising steadily. Pay differentials between the college

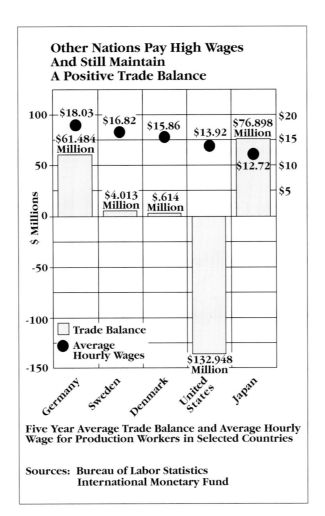

Other Nations Pay High Wages And Still Maintain A Positive Trade Balance

Five Year Average Trade Balance and Average Hourly Wage for Production Workers in Selected Countries

**Sources: Bureau of Labor Statistics
International Monetary Fund**

Each of these nations has maintained higher rates of productivity growth than the United States, and their living standards and real wages have been rising steadily.

educated and non-college educated are narrower, and the distribution of income is less skewed than in the United States.

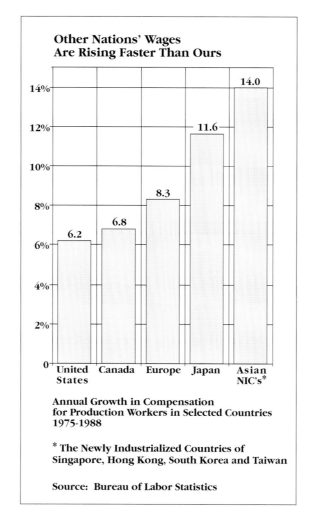

Other Nations' Wages Are Rising Faster Than Ours

Annual Growth in Compensation for Production Workers in Selected Countries 1975-1988

* The Newly Industrialized Countries of Singapore, Hong Kong, South Korea and Taiwan

Source: Bureau of Labor Statistics

How Are These Nations Coping?

These nations, while socially and culturally distinct, share a strong commitment to maintaining a high skill, high wage economy for all of their people. They also agree on certain fundamental principles concerning how to achieve this goal:

- Academic expectations are high for all young people. Both college bound and non-college bound students attain high standards of educational achievement.

- Well developed school-to-work transition programs provide young people with solid, recognized occupational skills.

- The skills of front-line workers are highly valued. Companies and governments are committed to providing lifelong training and employment opportunities to the average worker.

- Public labor market agencies provide valuable training, information and placement services for all workers.

- Government, business and the general society agree on the need to actively promote adoption of high performance work organizations.

Implementation varies widely in each of these countries. But each maintains coherent, highly systematic structures to stimulate both the supply of and the demand for highly skilled workers.

Basic Education

Every country we visited requires and makes an effort to ensure that its young people obtain basic proficiency in educational fundamentals (language, mathematics, geography, history, science and the arts).

Equal access to a quality education is critical for success. Disadvantaged areas (such as northern Sweden) and districts with problem populations get the most funds for education. National curricula and nationally or regionally standardized testing systems help set standards and reduce the variation in quality among schools. In Sweden, Denmark and Japan, students of mixed ability are generally kept in the same classes until they choose a career path at age 16. Tracking is uncommon.

The underlying assumption in all of these countries is that every student can be educated to be a productive worker in a high wage, high skill society.

Society makes it hard for students to fail. In Japan, students who fall behind are required to spend extra time on weekends, evenings and during vacations to catch up. In Sweden, students who drop out are pursued and strongly encouraged to study in alternative learning environments attached to local youth centers. In Germany, remedial education is provided in apprenticeship programs to ensure mastery of basic learning skills.

School-To-Work Transition

Extensive occupational preparation programs, combining general education with worksite training, provide foreign employers with high skilled, work ready youth and offer young people a smooth transition from school to working life.

In most of the countries we studied, schools begin early to prepare young people for working life. Students in Denmark, Germany and Sweden begin learning about occupations in the seventh grade from local employers and labor market representatives who visit the schools. Swedish children make field trips to workplaces and are required to complete 10 weeks of summer employment by age 16.

After they finish compulsory school at age 15 or 16, the majority of young people in Germany, Sweden and Denmark enter a two- to four-year professional program to prepare them for working life. In Germany, young people enter one of 380 formal apprenticeship programs and receive training in a company four days a week. In Sweden and Denmark, most of the instruction is provided in school, but students also participate in workplace training. Most of the

---

The important structural change for industry is in the mind. It's training, not machinery.

Swedish CEO

The underlying assumption in all of these countries is that every student can be educated to be a productive worker in a high wage, high skill society.

Extensive occupational preparation programs, combining general education with worksite training, provide foreign employers with high skilled, work ready youth and offer young people a smooth transition from school to working life.

After they finish compulsory school at age 15 or 16, the majority of young people in Germany, Sweden and Denmark enter a two- to four-year professional program to prepare them for working life.

programs are designed, if combined with the appropriate general education courses, to allow the student to continue on to college or a variety of higher technical and commercial programs.

Whether the training is provided mainly in the workplace or in the school, a common thread runs throughout the European workforce training systems:

- Study is provided in a wide range of occupations across industries, from auto repair and construction to food service and banking.

- Education generally combines school and work based learning and participants spend a certain portion of their studies training on the job.

- Companies and unions provide workplace training and maintain strong connections with the schools. Some firms in Sweden and Germany have even set up their own schools to attract highly qualified prospective job applicants.

- Representatives from relevant industry councils and unions design national standards for the programs, certify training providers, assess performance and certify completion.

- Students are assessed in performance based and written examinations. Those who meet the standards set by industry are recognized as skilled workers in the trade.

Employers, knowing that students who graduate from the system have the skills they seek, are glad to hire them. Students, seeing a direct relationship between school and work, are motivated to learn.

Unlike these central European systems, the Japanese emphasize general education. Although vocational schools are available to Japanese students, the majority complete high school in general education programs. Many companies hire for life, and Japanese employers, as a result, tend to place greater emphasis on a student's general learning ability and performance in school. Specific job related skills are provided by the company throughout the individual's working life.

Substantial orientation training, which may last for years, replaces the apprenticeship systems which exist in Europe. Virtually all Japanese students are handed over

Representatives from relevant industry councils and unions design national standards for the programs, certify training providers, assess performance and certify completion.

Employers, knowing that students who graduate from the system have the skills they seek, are glad to hire them. Students, seeing a direct relationship between school and work, are motivated to learn.

from a school 'family' to a work 'family' in a seamless transition requiring little external assistance.

We have no natural resources; no military power. We have only one resource: the inventive capacity of our brains. It has no limits. We must make use of it. We must educate, train, equip. In the near future, this mental power will become the most creative common good of all humanity.

Head, Japanese Federation of Economic Organizations (Keidranren)

The Labor Market System

All four countries maintain comprehensive public labor market systems to assist adult workers in finding appropriate training and employment.

In contrast to the United States, where public training and job information programs only serve a limited population, the systems abroad reach the majority. The foreign labor market services are carefully integrated, providing a 'one stop shop' for training and employment needs: employment placement, training and income maintenance for the unemployed and the exchange of labor market information. The systems are extremely well funded and play a critical role in their nation's overall economic strategies.

The labor market services are generally integrated under a single agency (or two related agencies, in the case of Sweden) and governed by a tripartite board of government, company and union representatives. The labor market service is funded either through the unemployment insurance system (Germany and Japan) or a special payroll tax (Sweden and Denmark).

Unemployment insurance systems in these countries are often coordinated with training programs. Typically, unemployment insurance is paid only as a stipend to those in training or, as a last resort, after training has taken place. In some cases, the training may be provided directly by a government training center, as in Sweden and Denmark, or the agency may pay for training offered by a private provider, as in Germany.

While in full-time training, workers are provided with the equivalent of the normal unemployment benefit to support themselves. Training is high quality and long term. For dislocated workers who are changing occupations, this may mean receiving training for two years or more.

A crucial responsibility of the public labor market agencies is to gather and disseminate information about the status of the labor market. Germany, Sweden, Denmark and Japan all employ elaborate market information services to guide policy and

All four countries maintain comprehensive public labor market systems to assist adult workers in finding appropriate training and employment.

. . . the systems abroad reach the majority. The foreign labor market services are carefully integrated, providing a 'one stop shop' for training and employment needs . . .

direct their more active programs. Typically, the information service gathers data on employers' needs in local labor markets, the skills which are available, and areas with surpluses and shortages. This information is then used by the service to determine what types of training to provide and to match unemployed workers to available jobs.

Company Training

Leading foreign firms spend up to six percent of payroll on training and devote a significant share of their effort to their front-line workers. Large German companies provide their workers with a wide range of free courses, either at company training centers or at outside institutions. Small German businesses pool their resources and operate external training centers through industry associations or local Chambers of Commerce. Japanese companies focus on shop floor training through formalized job rotation and instruction programs.

Government promotes in-company training to varying degrees in each of these countries. In Denmark, where the economy is dominated by small businesses, the government often provides training to companies free of charge. Sweden's national training centers and 'renewal funds' encourage companies to train. Companies are required to contribute a certain percentage of their payroll to the funds, but may later withdraw the money to finance training approved by the government and unions.

Leading foreign firms spend up to six percent of payroll on training and devote a significant share of their effort to their front-line workers.

I've toured a number of educational systems in Europe and the United States. The biggest question is always how to convince companies to spend the money on training. In Germany, this is not questioned. Everyone does it, and everyone knows how important it is for "Made in Germany."

German training director

Similar principles guide Singapore's Skills Development Fund and the Irish Levy-Grant system.

Organization Of Work

European and Japanese companies in most industries are further advanced than American companies in the development of high productivity forms of work organization. The leading firms, particularly those in manufacturing and retail, have now been experimenting with new processes and work cultures for a decade or more.

Swedish and Danish firms are perhaps the most advanced in adopting cooperative forms of work organization. Today, companies across many industries are using self-directed multi-skilled teams, expanding the skill content of jobs, providing continuing training and empowering workers to make day-to-day decisions. Workers are also consulted on all major investment and work organization decisions.

> **It used to take 700 people putting their hands on to build a single car. Now it takes 20.**
>
> *Volvo executive*

German work practices emphasize individual worker autonomy and the mastery of high level skills. Workers help plan the work organization and are consulted on major work related investments and plans.

Japanese firms stress collective worker participation in shop floor decisions, though in a paternalistic fashion. Broad based job rotation is commonplace, and managers spend most of their time on the shop floor. Japan has virtually abolished the hourly wage versus salary distinction and bases compensation for almost all employees on

> **We've tried to build a system which allows the people to control the materials, not vice versa.**
>
> *Former Volvo executive*

seniority. (Shop floor employees with levels of seniority comparable to the professional workforce may earn as much as salesmen and engineers.)

Particular work organization models vary by country, but the outcome is the same: greater responsibility and earning power for the average worker.

Why Are Foreign Companies Choosing High Skills?

Foreign managers do not adopt new forms of work organization because they are more altruistic or more far-sighted than American firms. Most foreign companies choose high productivity models in response to a variety of external and labor market pressures.

National full employment policies, tight labor markets, government labor regulations, strong union movements, high wages and a highly skilled workforce all provide incentives for foreign employers to choose the high productivity path.

In Japan, Sweden and Singapore, official public commitments to full employment limit the ability of employers to lay off workers. These policies create a tight labor market, making it difficult for employers to attract new employees. Broader job definitions, attractive career paths and better work conditions can give them an edge in hiring.

In Sweden, Denmark and Germany, companies are required by law to consult with unions before they can lay off workers. Throughout Europe, requirements of timely notice and severance pay strongly discourage layoffs. Employers therefore have strong incentives to invest in their workers and provide training and good career tracks.

European and Japanese companies in most industries are further advanced than American companies in the development of high productivity forms of work organization . . . Particular work organization models vary by country, but the outcome is the same: greater responsibility and earning power for the average worker.

. . . the higher education and skill levels of foreign workers make it both necessary and possible for foreign companies to adopt new forms of work organization.

But higher education levels also mean that workers are less willing to tolerate traditional forms of work.

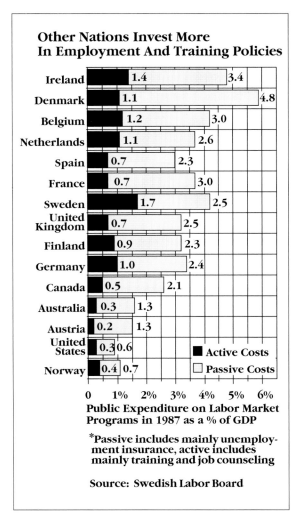

Other Nations Invest More In Employment And Training Policies

Nation	Active Costs	Passive Costs
Ireland	1.4	3.4
Denmark	1.1	4.8
Belgium	1.2	3.0
Netherlands	1.1	2.6
Spain	0.7	2.3
France	0.7	3.0
Sweden	1.7	2.5
United Kingdom	0.7	2.5
Finland	0.9	2.3
Germany	1.0	2.4
Canada	0.5	2.1
Australia	0.3	1.3
Austria	0.2	1.3
United States	0.3	0.6
Norway	0.4	0.7

■ Active Costs
□ Passive Costs

0   1%   2%   3%   4%   5%   6%

Public Expenditure on Labor Market Programs in 1987 as a % of GDP

*Passive includes mainly unemployment insurance, active includes mainly training and job counseling

Source: Swedish Labor Board

High wage levels, due in part to union pressure and national income policies, also force companies to achieve higher levels of productivity either through increased training or new forms of work organization.

Finally, the higher education and skill levels of foreign workers make it both necessary and possible for foreign companies to adopt new forms of work organization. Strong occupational preparation allows workers to handle more complex work assignments and greater front-line responsibilities. But higher education levels also mean that workers are less willing to tolerate traditional forms of work.

Swedish education reforms in the 1960's that drastically raised education requirements also precipitated high rates of absenteeism in Swedish factories. Young workers, bored by traditional factory work, opted to stay at home. This caused manufacturing employers, in particular, to reorganize work in order to increase job content, with the aim of attracting workers.

Them And Us

While these nations differ in economy and culture, they share an approach to the education and training of their workers and to high productivity work organization that we lack:

- They insist that virtually all of their students reach a high educational standard. We do not.
- They provide 'professionalized' education to non-college educated workers to prepare them for their trades and to ease their school-to-work transition. We do not.

This is the reason for the great expansion of further education in Germany right now. Germany is fighting to hold a quality edge over countries like Korea and Japan — not so much with the United States. The problem with the United States is that there are too many people in college and not enough qualified workers. The United States has outstanding universities, but it is missing its middle. Too much training takes place on the job, and therefore is too unsystematic.

German executive

- They operate comprehensive labor market systems which combine training, labor market information, job search and income maintenance for the unemployed. We do not.

- They support company based training through financing schemes based on general revenue or payroll tax. We do not.

- They have national consensus on the importance of moving to high productivity forms of work organization and building high wage economies. We do not.

America stands out among advanced nations as having a unique set of approaches to education, training, school-to-work transition and overall labor market policy.

Our approaches have served us well in the past. They will not serve us well in the future.

America stands out among advanced nations as having a unique set of approaches to education, training, school-to-work transition and overall labor market policy. Our approaches have served us well in the past. They will not serve us well in the future.

8

THE CHOICE

Americans are unwittingly making a choice. It is a choice that most of us would probably not make were we aware of its consequences. Yet every day, that choice is becoming more difficult to reverse. It is a choice which undermines the American dream of economic opportunity for all. It is a choice that will lead to an America where 30 percent of our people may do well — at least for a while — but the other 70 percent will see their dreams slip away.

The choice that America faces is a choice between high skills and low wages. Gradually, silently, we are choosing low wages.

The choice is being made by companies that cut wages to remain competitive. It is being made by public officials who fail to prepare our children to be productive workers. Ultimately, we are all making the choice by silently accepting this course.

We still have time to make the other choice — one that will lead us to a more prosperous future — a choice for high skills, not low wages. To make this choice, we must fundamentally change our approach to work and education:

- Today, we demand too little of those students not headed for college.

  Tomorrow, we must demand high performance from all students, even those not going on to college.

- Today, we shrug our shoulders as over 20 percent of our students — more than 50 percent in the inner cities — drop out of schools.

  Tomorrow, we must ensure that all young people get the education they need to succeed.

- Today, we blame schools for not providing the type of workers employers want, yet employers are rarely involved in student's education and training.

  Tomorrow, we must share responsibility with the schools for defining standards of professional competence and take the lead in helping students cross the bridge from school to work.

The choice that America faces is a choice between high skills and low wages. Gradually, silently, we are choosing low wages.

The choice is being made by companies that cut wages to remain competitive. It is being made by public officials who fail to prepare our children to be productive workers. Ultimately, we are all making the choice by silently accepting this course. We still have time to make the other choice . . . a choice for high skills, not low wages.

We will be successful if our work kindles a debate that leads to action, however formulated, that sets America firmly on a high skill, high wage course.

- Today, we stop educating our non-college bound youth at 18 — they must sink or swim with the skills they have acquired by that age.

  Tomorrow, we must create a means for students not going to college and for people already in the workforce to acquire and renew the technical and professional skills they need for high productivity work.

- Today, we limit our public labor policies to temporary income maintenance and minimal training for the poor and unemployed.

  Tomorrow, we must expand those policies to embrace skill development for all workers.

- Today, we don't seem to care if companies choose to compete by cutting wages or by increasing productivity and quality.

  Tomorrow, we must provide incentives for the high productivity, high quality choice.

Our Commission members share a deep concern about the future that America is choosing. If America is to remain prosperous, fundamental changes are needed in the way work is organized and in the way we educate and train our people.

We hope and expect that others will examine our proposals carefully. But success, in our view, is not necessarily tied to the adoption of our precise plan. We will be successful if our work kindles a debate that leads to action, however formulated, that sets America firmly on a high skill, high wage course.

9

THE FOUNDATION SKILLS

Recommendation #1

A new educational performance standard should be set for all students, to be met by age 16. This standard should be established nationally and benchmarked to the highest in the world.

All of our students should meet a national standard of educational excellence by age 16, or soon thereafter, which will equal or exceed the highest similar standard in the world for students of that age. A student passing a series of performance based assessments that incorporate the standard should be awarded a Certificate of Initial Mastery.

In order to adequately prepare our young people for working life, we must first see that they acquire the educational skills necessary to become effective players in a highly productive society.

The establishment of a system of national standards and assessment would ensure that every student leaves compulsory school with a demonstrated ability to read, write, compute and perform at world-class levels in general school subjects (mathematics, physical and natural sciences, technology, history, geography, politics, economics and English). Students should also have

exhibited a capacity to learn, think, work effectively alone and in groups and solve problems.

Among other things, the Certificate of Initial Mastery would certify labor market readiness, and a mastery of the basic skills necessary for high productivity employment. The same Certificate would also be required for entry into all subsequent forms of education, including college preparatory and certified professional and technical programs.

The assessment system would establish objective standards for students and educators, motivate students and give employers an objective means to assess the capabilities of job applicants.

The Certificate of Initial Mastery would not indicate the completion of a student's formal education. Rather, for the vast majority of students, this achievement would serve as a foundation for more advanced forms of education or training.

Effort Based Education And Assessment

The United States is the most over-tested and under-examined nation in the world. Most of the tests that American students take —

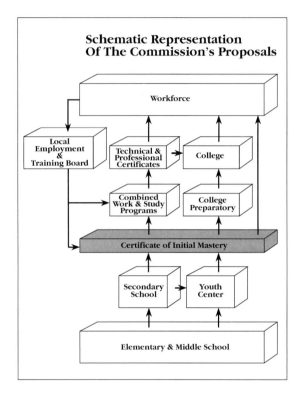

Schematic Representation Of The Commission's Proposals

Workforce

Local Employment & Training Board

Technical & Professional Certificates

College

Combined Work & Study Programs

College Preparatory

Certificate of Initial Mastery

Secondary School

Youth Center

Elementary & Middle School

All of our students should meet a national standard of educational excellence by age 16, or soon thereafter, which will equal or exceed the highest similar standard in the world for students of that age. A student passing a series of performance based assessments that incorporate the standard should be awarded a Certificate of Initial Mastery.

The assessment system would establish objective standards for students and educators, motivate students and give employers an objective means to assess the capabilities of job applicants.

standardized achievement tests and college entrance tests — are deliberately decoupled from the school curriculum. Teachers are not supposed to prepare students directly for these tests, and students are not supposed to study for them (except in 'cram courses' that few believe have lasting educational value).

As a result of this testing system, American education does not clearly reward academic effort on the part of either teachers or students.

An examination based assessment system would fundamentally change this situation. At the heart of such a system would be a series of performance based examinations for which students can explicitly prepare. (The type of assessment system we have in mind is detailed in Supporting Information I.)

A Cumulative Assessment System

The assessment system should allow students to collect credentials over a period of years, perhaps beginning as early as entrance into the middle school. This kind of cumulative assessment has several advantages over a single series of examinations:

- It would help to organize and motivate students over an extended period of time. Rather than preparing for a far-off examination (the form and demands of which a 12-year-old can only dimly imagine), students could begin early to collect specific certifications.

- It would provide multiple opportunities for success rather than a single high-stakes moment of possible failure. Cumulative certificates would greatly enhance the opportunity for the undereducated and unmotivated to achieve high educational standards. All could earn credentials at their own pace, as the criteria for any specific credential would not vary, regardless of the student's age.

- It would allow students who are not performing well in the mainstream education system to earn their credentials under other institutional auspices.

An Independent Examining Organization

To set the assessment standards and certification procedures, we recommend the establishment of an independent national examining organization that broadly represents educators, employers and the citizenry at large.

The organization should be authorized to convene working commissions in a variety of knowledge and skill areas to help train judges, set and assess standards and conduct examinations. The organization should be independent of schools and school systems and protected from political pressures.

10

UNIVERSAL MASTERY OF THE FOUNDATION SKILLS

Recommendation #2

The states should take responsibility for assuring that virtually all students achieve a Certificate of Initial Mastery. Through the new local Employment and Training Boards, the states, with Federal assistance, should create and fund alternative learning environments for those who cannot attain the Certificate of Initial Mastery in regular schools.

It is not enough to establish a high performance standard. It is essential that everyone meets it. Above all, we must avoid creating a system of educational 'haves' and 'have nots' in which some students attain the Certificate of Initial Mastery while others are permanently relegated to the backwaters of our society. The purpose of the Certificate is to improve the lifetime education and employment opportunities of all students, not to exacerbate the problems that already exist.

Not all students will meet the standard at the age of 16. Some will achieve it earlier. They should have the option of advancing immediately to further education or training. Others may remain in school until age 18

before they earn their Certificate of Initial Mastery. But some will drop out of school along the way. What should happen to them?

Local Youth Centers: The Dropout Recovery System

We recommend that the states, through the new local Employment and Training Boards (described in a later chapter), establish local Youth Centers. These Centers would be legally responsible to the Boards for all young people between the ages of 14 and 21 who have left school before acquiring their Certificates of Initial Mastery. Ideally, there should be a Youth Center in every community or neighborhood.

The first priority of the Youth Center would be to ensure that every young person attains the Certificate. The Center should provide a supportive, family-like environment. Young people would have year-round access to basic education in alternative settings, employment and career counseling, work experience and job placement. The Center would provide these services by maintaining strong liaisons with employers and connections with the full range of

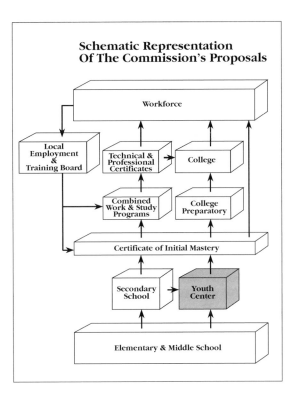

Schematic Representation Of The Commission's Proposals

We recommend that the states, through the new local Employment and Training Boards . . . establish local Youth Centers . . . The first priority of the Youth Center would be to ensure that every young person attains the Certificate.

. . . work experience and job placement. The Center would provide these services by maintaining strong liaisons with employers . . .

The Center should employ alternate learning techniques that are responsive to different learning styles. Many of the best existing programs emphasize learning by doing — often on a job . . .

community health and social service agencies. A strong mentoring network would be fostered to provide positive role models for the Center's participants.

A Center might extend its services in a number of ways. At one end of the spectrum, the Center could provide all or most of the core services itself. Or, it could contract with a range of providers, including public, private, for-profit and not-for-profit organizations (including schools) to supply many of its services. Some programs already in existence can point the way (see Supporting Information II).

The Center should employ alternate learning techniques that are responsive to different learning styles. Many of the best existing programs emphasize learning by doing — often on a job — as well as use of computer based instruction. These techniques and many others could be adapted to suit individual circumstances.

Building The Connection Between Work And Education For Young People Who Do Not Have Their Certificates

Today, the motivation to achieve in high school is often overshadowed by the money a job can provide. Students who drop out of school, or who merely maintain a physical presence long enough to obtain a diploma

(doing as little work as possible), often get jobs to have spending money. They see no economic benefit to more schoolwork. They are often right.

The most effective way to get young people to achieve their educational qualifications is to establish clear signals that their education will have genuine value and to create positive consequences for effort and success. Vague homilies on the importance of learning will not work. The lack of any clear, direct connection between education and employment opportunities for most young people is one of the most devastating aspects of the existing system.

That kind of connection will only occur for many students in the Youth Centers if local employers organize to provide job opportunities for them. Business compacts and individual companies across the nation already give preference in hiring to young people who stay in school.

We strongly urge extension of such initiatives to establish employment and training options for Youth Center enrollees.

Guaranteeing the right to a good education to every young American and providing positive links between educational achievement and jobs are essential to the creation of an educated nation. However, we recognize that some young people will still not exercise their right. Thus, success must also depend on placing an obligation on young people to learn.

Once Youth Centers are established, we propose that the child labor laws be amended to make the granting of work permits to young people up to age 18 contingent on either their possession of a Certificate of Initial Mastery, or their enrollment in a program leading to the Certificate.

At first glance, this may seem draconian. But, in the long run, this requirement will benefit our youth and ultimately the nation. If our future workers do not possess the education and skills signified by the Certificate of Initial Mastery, they will be condemned to dead-end jobs that leave them in poverty even if they are working. The $4 per hour they can earn at age 16 might seem appealing compared to no earnings, but if that is all they are equipped to earn at age 30, the appeal will be gone.

In high unemployment areas, where the prospect of earning money while going to the Youth Center program is slight, we suggest that the states and Federal government, through the Youth Center, provide paid work-study arrangements. (Safeguards can be created to prevent displacement of the existing adult workforce and to protect labor standards.) In certain cases where such work would create particular hardships, stipends for needy students should be considered.

Preschool Preparation And School Restructuring

No nation can expect to meet a world education standard when one out of five of its children lives in poverty. That problem will not be eliminated overnight. In the meantime, it is essential to address the worst effects of poverty among children. Much can be accomplished through the extension of effective child development programs to more children in need, a problem on which the administration and the Congress have made a start. It will also be critically important to improve the health of young, low-income children, especially the growing number born addicted to drugs. We have not studied these problems in detail, but we recognize that our aspirations require their solution.

To say that we cannot reach a world education standard without addressing the problem of poverty is not, however, to say that the schools cannot be held accountable for poor student performance. The record shows that some inner city and rural schools serving very poor children produce high levels of student achievement.

If standards are raised and nothing is done to improve our schools, the Youth Centers might become catchment areas for a swiftly growing number of students. This is not our intention. The success of our pro-

The lack of any clear, direct connection between education and employment opportunities for most young people is one of the most devastating aspects of the existing system. That kind of connection will only occur for many students in the Youth Centers if local employers organize to provide job opportunities for them.

Once Youth Centers are established, we propose that the child labor laws be amended to make the granting of work permits to young people up to age 18 contingent on either their possession of a Certificate of Initial Mastery, or their enrollment in a program leading to the Certificate.

Not until there are real rewards for school staffs whose students succeed and real consequences for those whose students do not can we safely assume that everything possible is being done to help all children succeed in school.

posals will depend on the schools doing a much better job of educating all students. High standards alone will not ensure that outcome.

The schools — like our businesses — also need to be restructured for high performance by pushing decisions down to the school staff and then holding the staff accountable for student performance. As matters now stand, teachers often lack the discretion they need to be able to bring everyone up to a high standard. But they also lack the incentive to make the effort. Not until there are real rewards for school staffs whose students succeed and real consequences for those whose students do not can we safely assume that everything possible is being done to help all children succeed in school.

Incentives For Schools To Retain Potential Dropouts

Many school districts are making substantial efforts to improve the education of low income students but have little success simply because they lack the necessary funds. A number of the countries we visited address this problem by making sure that those school districts serving the poorest children and those in sparsely populated areas are funded at the highest levels. Their

objective is not to provide 'foundation' aid that can be supplemented by those communities in the best position to do so, as in the United States, but rather to be sure that everyone has what it takes to get up to the same high performance standard.

If the United States followed these countries' examples, it is very likely that enrollment in the Youth Centers would fall as the districts became better able to meet the needs of students in trouble.

Funding The Youth Centers

The Youth Centers we have proposed must have the funds they need to succeed. School districts would be required to notify the nearest Youth Center about any student who drops out. The school district would transfer to the Youth Center the average per-pupil expenditure (including all state and Federal funds) that the school would have received for that student. Payment would continue until the student receives the Certificate of Initial Mastery or reaches age 21, whichever comes first.

This structure creates a powerful incentive for schools and governments to develop programs to retain and educate their students properly the first time.

Dropouts are expensive for America. A high percentage of student dropouts abuse drugs, commit crimes, are unemployed or must rely on welfare. Many become teenage parents. More than 60 percent of the people in our prisons are high-school dropouts. On average, it costs more than $16,000 per year to keep prisoners housed compared with less than $4,300 for a year of high school.

In 1989 approximately 800,000 16-year-olds dropped out of high school. To support them in the schools would have cost about $3.4 billion per year.

To educate those dropouts in Youth Centers would probably be more expensive because many have special needs. If we added a premium of 20 percent for every dropout attending a Youth Center program, and if it took two extra years in a Youth Center to attain the Certificate of Initial Mastery, the Youth Center system would cost about $8.2 billion per year.

This is a small price to pay to assure that every dropout in the nation acquires the skills and competencies necessary to lead a productive work life. If we hope to remain a competitive and productive economy, we cannot afford to lose 20 to 25 percent of our future workers; we must begin taking responsibility for them.

Who is going to pay? We have proposed that the school districts do so, but it is unreasonable to expect beleaguered inner cities and rural communities to pay the additional costs of dropout recovery without help from outside the community. That help should be forthcoming from both state and Federal governments. Some may come from reallocating funds that now go to wealthier districts, but the most likely source will be new revenues. Either way, the sum, though substantial, is small in relation to the certain gain.

If we hope to remain a competitive and productive economy, we cannot afford to lose 20 to 25 percent of our future workers; we must begin taking responsibility for them.

11

TECHNICAL AND PROFESSIONAL EDUCATION

Recommendation #3

A comprehensive system of Technical and Professional Certificates and associate's degrees should be created for the majority of our students and adult workers who do not pursue a baccalaureate degree.

Our goal is to establish a structure that will give our front-line workers the systematic skills, professional qualifications and respect that their counterparts enjoy in other countries.

The system we propose would also provide a clear structure for young people to make a smooth transition from school to work. It would offer them clear routes to a variety of career qualifications, opportunity for work based learning and an alternative path to college.

Technical and Professional Certificates would be offered across the entire range of service and manufacturing occupations. A student could earn the first occupation-specific certificate after completing two to four years of combined work and study, depending upon the field. A sequence of

advanced certificates, attesting to mastery of more complex skills, would be available and could be obtained throughout one's career.

This proposal contains four elements:

1. Performance based assessment standards should be established for jobs covering the broad range of occupations in the United States that do not require a baccalaureate degree. Achievement of standards would result in awards of Technical and Professional Certificates and associate's degrees for various mastery levels. The standards, at least equal to those set by other advanced industrialized countries, should be set by national committees convened by the Secretary of Labor.

2. High schools, community colleges, proprietary schools and other educational and training institutions should be encouraged to offer courses leading to the Technical and Professional Certificates and associate's degrees. Programs and their providers should be accredited by state boards of higher and vocational education.

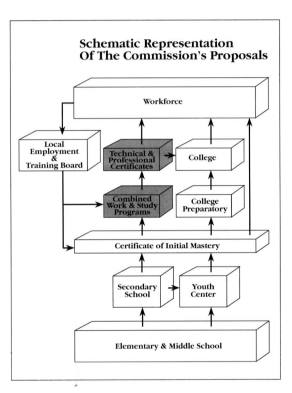

Schematic Representation Of The Commission's Proposals

A National Board for Professional and Technical Standards should be established ... [to] ... develop a national system of industry based standards and certifications of mastery across a broad range of occupations.

Industry and trade based committees appointed by the Board would develop standards for each industry and trade.

3. Employers should provide part-time work and training as part of the curriculum in each certification course and reward those who attain the certificates with higher quality jobs and better pay.

4. The states and the Federal government should furnish four years of financing to all Americans to allow them to pursue education beyond the Certificate of Initial Mastery at some point in their adult lives.

A system of industry based skill certifications has a number of attractive features. It would facilitate communication between schools and industry about employer and union expectations and goals. By setting criteria for hiring, it would help employers find qualified applicants. For employees, it would establish clear knowledge and skill based standards for career progression, help prevent hiring discrimination and improve the transferability of skills. Finally, for government, a system of skill based certification would offer an independent means of assessing the competence of training deliverers.

The Certification System

A National Board for Professional and Technical Standards should be established by the Secretary of Labor with the cooperation of the Secretaries of Commerce and Education. This Board, composed of distinguished representatives of employers, unions, education and advocacy groups would develop a national system of industry based standards and certifications of mastery across a broad range of occupations.

Industry and trade based committees appointed by the Board would develop standards for each industry and trade. Each Committee would build upon existing certification procedures, and develop a single coherent and internationally competitive set of assessments to guide career progression within each industry or trade.

The Program

The occupational certification programs would be open both to students (as soon as they receive their Certificates of Initial Mastery) and adult workers. The assessment standard for a program would be the same for both adults and students, although the delivery mechanism and curricular details might vary.

Each occupational program should combine school and work based learning and balance general education and industry specific requirements. Clear qualifications and career progressions should be established within each occupation.

With appropriate labor standards and other safeguards, the work component of these programs could provide industry with the temporary and part-time workers they seek, allowing them to give their full-time workers greater stability. For students, these jobs would provide valuable work experience and some income.

The system should offer mobility, both horizontally among occupations and vertically into options for further training or study. Above all, it must be designed to avoid dead ends. Young people who succeed in one of these programs should receive a high-school diploma or an associate's degree, and should qualify to enter college or a variety of advanced technical or professional programs.

A sample four-year curriculum to prepare manufacturing professionals could include English, math, history, statistics, computer programming, communications, physics, chemistry and operations analysis. It could also include industry specific subjects such as introductory courses in mechanical, electrical, chemical and electronic machinery; instrumentation and testing procedures; cost accounting; industrial design; and inventory, process and statistical quality control.

A young person who receives a Certificate of Initial Mastery might pursue the program in high school, a local community college or in a 'two-plus-two' program.

Similarly, individuals seeking a career in retail could also pursue a three-year program combining general courses with occupation-specific learning. General courses might include introductory computer programming, English and foreign languages, accounting, public speaking, psychology and business. Occupation-specific courses could include retailing, inventory control, customer relations, ordering systems, merchandising and marketing. The program might also include options for specialization in certain products. A program in clothing retailing, for example, might include courses on how different types of clothing are manufactured, fabric characteristics and care, fashion design and so on.

Funding Technical And Professional Education

The Commission believes strongly that our society should provide the resources to allow all students to pursue these Technical and Professional Certificates. No student should be discouraged from doing so for financial reasons.

The vast majority of students entering these technical and professional certification programs would do so around their junior year in high school at age 16.

A substantial amount — more than $35 billion — is already being spent on the education and training of our 16- to 19-year-old population.

All states guarantee free education to students in their junior and senior years of high school. These funds could be used for the first two years of college preparation courses or professional and technical education beyond the Certificate of Initial Mastery for all students.

The system should offer mobility, both horizontally among occupations and vertically into options for further training or study. Above all, it must be designed to avoid dead ends.

In addition, some states also heavily subsidize attendance at community colleges and universities for the 40 to 50 percent of their citizens taking post-high-school courses. These funds could be used to finance the Technical and Professional Certificate programs we propose.

But the current financing systems for post-secondary students who are not studying full time for a baccalaureate degree are inadequate and uneven. The Commission believes these students deserve the same kind of support that four-year college students receive. A mechanism should be created that provides four years of funding beyond the Certificate of Initial Mastery for everyone. That mechanism could make use of the funds already available, but it should provide a means to meet the needs of every candidate for Technical and Professional Certificates.

The needed funds could result from a modification and extension of existing programs or from new sources.

At one extreme, a 'GI Bill' system could be funded from general revenues to guarantee everyone four free years of education beyond the Certificate of Initial Mastery. Studies indicate that the 'GI Bill' paid for itself many times over in increased income for America.

At the other extreme, a self-financing scheme could be created whereby the government would loan all students the funds for post-secondary professional, technical or college education and then recoup the loan through a small surcharge on an individual's income taxes over many years.

We call upon the National Center on Education and the Economy to convene a panel of experts to make recommendations for funding the system we propose.

The specific method of funding chosen is not as important as the establishment of a means to provide universal access to serious professional and technical training for our non-college educated workforce.

12

LIFELONG LEARNING AND HIGH PERFORMANCE WORK ORGANIZATIONS

Recommendation #4

All employers should be given incentives and assistance to invest in the further education and training of their workers and to pursue high productivity forms of work organization.

America's productivity in the 1990's will climb only if the strategies of American employers are redrafted to include serious investments in work reorganization and worker training. While many employers talk about human resource issues, too few consider them to be fundamental to their organization's success.

To make full use of the productive potential of our workforce and to encourage the use of high productivity models of work organization, we recommend that employers be provided with financial incentives to train their workers and with the technical assistance necessary to move toward higher productivity work organizations.

Other countries are driven to pursue high productivity work because public laws make it difficult to pay low wages and lay off workers. National full-employment policies, stringent severance and layoff notification laws, high minimum wage laws and statutes requiring union approval of management actions all motivate foreign companies to invest in their workforces. Since this is a Commission on workforce skills, we have not addressed these broader policies directly.

However, other nations are also driven to high performance work organizations by laws that require companies to invest directly in the training of their workers (see Supporting Information IV). In many advanced industrial nations, laws require companies to spend between one percent and three and a half percent of their payrolls on formal training programs (beyond normal on-the-job training).

Because this is required, companies are encouraged to think about how to make the best use of these funds to develop skills.

In this country, only a handful of our companies invest in training. Those who do not, fear that such investments will be wasted, because trained employees will be

America's productivity in the 1990's will climb only if the strategies of American employers are redrafted to include serious investments in work reorganization and worker training.

. . . we recommend that employers be provided with financial incentives to train their workers and with the technical assistance necessary to move toward higher productivity work organizations.

Initially, employers would be required to spend approximately one percent of payroll on education and training . . .

Employers failing to meet this target would be required to contribute approximately one percent of payroll to a national Skills Development Fund.

All companies, organizations and institutions, regardless of size or type of business, including local and state governments and schools, would be required to participate.

hired away. Others simply do not see the value of significant training investment, because of the way they use their workers.

Compulsion is never a popular approach to public policy. Playing copy-cat with the policies of other countries is not what made this country great. However, the small minority of our companies that do invest in training, either out of competitive necessity or simply because it makes good business sense, are not being treated fairly. They are carrying the national training imperative on their backs.

The overriding issue is not the economic survival of a few employers; it is the economic security of an entire workforce. The nation will not compete effectively unless all employers participate in a set of financial incentives to train their workers.

An Incentive For Training And Work Reorganization

American employers on average spend slightly more than one percent on formal training. However, the distribution of spending is highly skewed. A small percentage of firms spend more than two percent, while the vast majority are well below one percent.

We recommend that the Federal government require all employers to spend a minimum amount of funds annually to send their employees through certified education and training programs. In unionized workplaces, companies and unions should jointly negotiate and administer the training programs.

Initially, employers would be required to spend approximately one percent of payroll on education and training (with the amount increasing progressively over the decade). Employers in many foreign countries are already required to invest a minimum of one percent in employee training. Companies should fund training for frontline workers in proportion to their total representation in the firm's workforce.

Employers failing to meet this target would be required to contribute approximately one percent of payroll to a national Skills Development Fund. The exact amount for each organization would be calculated as a specific payment per worker, in order to ensure sufficient resources to train lower paid workers.

The Skills Development Fund would be used to train temporary, part-time, dislocated and disadvantaged workers whose training employers would probably not underwrite.

All companies, organizations and institutions, regardless of size or type of business, including local and state governments and schools, would be required to participate. The Commission feels strongly that this expenditure should come from employer, not employee, contributions. The contribution would thus give employers an incentive to reorganize work to take advantage of the higher skill levels for which they are paying.

Until the various certificate programs we propose are implemented, employers should be allowed to use their training allotment for tuition and instructional costs for any type of organized instruction (not including direct efforts on the job). The program should be approved by the union if there is one.

After the occupational certification programs are established, however, we recommend that only accredited courses that form part of a formal certification program or a college degree program be counted toward the employer's minimum training obligation.

Tying acceptable expenditures to certificate programs makes the expenditure easy to monitor, ensures that funds are not being spent on frivolous activities and helps employees obtain skills that have broad application.

Developing employees' skills, however, does not necessarily lead to smooth or successful reorganization of work. For this reason, the Commission recommends that up to 15 percent of the funds be used for expenses associated with efforts to redesign work. Acceptable activities might include research and development on competency based training or on high productivity work reorganization.

Each year, employers would be asked to certify that they had met these training and education requirements, perhaps as part of the unemployment insurance tax form. No new bureaucracy would be needed and the reporting requirement would be minimal. California and Rhode Island, among other states, are already collecting funds for training through the unemployment insurance program.

This proposal may appear burdensome to small companies that do not compete internationally or perceive no need for training. But the most equitable initiative is one that treats all companies and institutions uniformly. If employers cannot or will not make the necessary investments to train their workers today, the government will be forced to train them tomorrow. A skilled, productive workforce benefits our nation's economic well-being. It is everyone's responsibility.

For that reason, the Commission feels that the proposed method for financing further training is fair and reasonable, however, other proposals might also be used.

For example, companies below a certain size might be exempted from this obligation and training for their employees could be provided through the Skills Development Fund. Another possibility is to use public funds to finance continuing education and training. A third alternative would be to

. . . only accredited courses that form part of a formal certification program or a college degree program [should] be counted toward the employer's minimum training obligation.

. . . up to 15 percent of the funds . . . [could] . . . be used for expenses associated with efforts to redesign work.

*Reorganizing toward higher
productivity forms of work
may seem risky and even
companies that are
committed to this path often
lack the information or
technical expertise necessary
to accomplish the task. This
is especially true for the
nation's small businesses.*

*We therefore make two
proposals. First, that a
national information and
technical service be
established to provide
support to companies in the
reorganization of work.
Second, that national quality
awards be expanded to
recognize more best-practice
companies.*

create an individual training account financed by companies and by the government.

Each method has advantages and disadvantages. Here again, the details of the finance plan are less important to this Commission than the necessity of developing some means of investing in our front-line workers. Virtually every advanced industrial nation uses one or another of these methods to create a substantial fund to support the continuing education and training of workers. We are one of the few with no method — and no fund — at all.

Incentives To Create High Performance Work Organizations

Reorganizing toward higher productivity forms of work may seem risky and even companies that are committed to this path often lack the information or technical expertise necessary to accomplish the task. This is especially true for the nation's small businesses.

We therefore make two proposals. First, that a national information and technical service be established to provide support to companies in the reorganization of work. Second, that national quality awards be expanded to recognize more best-practice companies.

Technical Assistance For Employers

The United States Department of Commerce should establish a National Clearinghouse for the Reorganization of Work and Workforce Skills Development. The Clearinghouse would be responsible for coordinating all Federal assistance to employers and should work closely with the Departments of Labor, Defense, and Education to:

- Disseminate information on successful forms of work reorganization across industries and types of businesses.

- Promote and help coordinate educational visits to successful high performance work sites.

- Provide a one-stop shop for firms seeking general or specific guidance and solutions to challenges encountered during the transition to new forms of work.

- Distribute examples of best-practice companies, as well as materials from other agencies, such as the Department of Defense's training methodologies and instructional programs.

- Encourage partnerships among state, local and private sector groups.

The National Science Foundation should be given a mission to improve workplace practices through the development and application of new technology.

We endorse the establishment of a civilian technology agency in the Department of Commerce. Such an agency would, among many other functions, have the responsibility to help companies organize work so as to make the most efficient and effective use of new technologies.

Federal laboratories in several Cabinet departments should be asked to devote greater efforts to the commercial applications of the technologies in which they are involved and to training companies in implementing high productivity work organizations related to those technologies.

The 1988 Omnibus Trade and Competitiveness Act established three manufacturing technology centers and provided for assistance to state technology centers. These, too, could become a focal point for assessing and disseminating effective approaches to the organization of work to businesses interested in making the most effective use of new manufacturing technologies.

Quality Awards

To focus national attention on the issue of work reorganization, awards programs designed to recognize and promote quality, excellence, productivity and improved workplace environments should be expanded.

The Malcolm Baldrige National Quality Award contributes significantly to the national awareness of quality and the reorganization of work. The Senate productivity awards and state quality awards also play important roles. We recommend expansion of these awards to recognize more best-practice companies and institutions.

The Department of Labor has recently established a new award to recognize excellence in upgrading the quality of the American workforce. We strongly urge that, as part of its criteria, the award include changes in the organization of work and their effect on worklife and employee productivity.

Federal laboratories in several Cabinet departments should be asked to devote greater efforts to the commercial applications of the technologies in which they are involved and to training companies in implementing high productivity work organizations related to those technologies.

13

AND A SYSTEM TO PULL IT TOGETHER

Recommendation #5

A system of Employment and Training Boards should be established by Federal and state governments, together with local leadership, to organize and oversee the new school-to-work transition programs and training systems we propose.

In this report, we have compared American educational and training programs to those in other industrial countries. In every case, we have found that somewhere in this country, a state, city or institution is doing something as interesting, as imaginative and as effective as anything done anywhere in the world.

What is missing is a cohesive system. What we lack, and what many of our competitors have, is a means of joining all the pieces together into one seamless web.

Our preceding proposals lay the foundation for a cohesive, high performance education and training system. We would reorganize the current array of programs and institutions into a streamlined system based on two sets of goals:

- We expect our standards for the Certificate of Initial Mastery to drive a system of work preparation designed to bring every American, youth or adult, up to a high level of foundation skills. These standards should be applied to every program or institution concerned with basic education or literacy. This would include our current K-12 system of education, the alternative Youth Center system we propose and remedial programs for youth and adults operated through a variety of public programs.

- We expect our standards of technical and professional mastery to drive a system of occupational education and training designed to allow a majority of American workers to thrive on new technologies and work processes. These standards would apply to corporate training and to programs in high schools, community colleges and proprietary schools. Thus, no matter where the training took place,

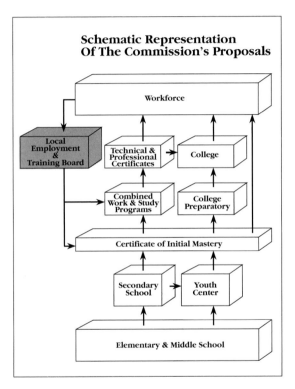

Schematic Representation Of The Commission's Proposals

Progressing Through The New Structure:
Four Examples

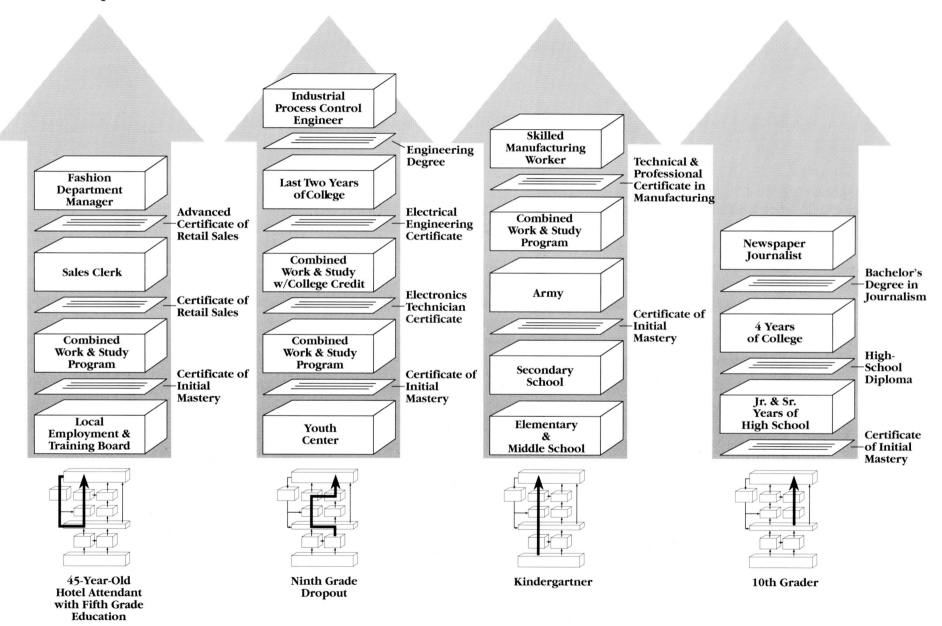

Example 1 — 45-Year-Old Hotel Attendant with Fifth Grade Education

- Local Employment & Training Board
- Certificate of Initial Mastery
- Combined Work & Study Program
- Certificate of Retail Sales
- Sales Clerk
- Advanced Certificate of Retail Sales
- Fashion Department Manager

Example 2 — Ninth Grade Dropout

- Youth Center
- Certificate of Initial Mastery
- Combined Work & Study Program
- Electronics Technician Certificate
- Combined Work & Study w/College Credit
- Electrical Engineering Certificate
- Last Two Years of College
- Engineering Degree
- Industrial Process Control Engineer

Example 3 — Kindergartner

- Elementary & Middle School
- Secondary School
- Army
- Certificate of Initial Mastery
- Combined Work & Study Program
- Technical & Professional Certificate in Manufacturing
- Skilled Manufacturing Worker

Example 4 — 10th Grader

- Jr. & Sr. Years of High School
- Certificate of Initial Mastery
- High-School Diploma
- 4 Years of College
- Bachelor's Degree in Journalism
- Newspaper Journalist

employers and individuals would have confidence in its quality and its transferability.

The certification systems we propose, and the education and training initiatives they drive, should be linked to labor market information and to job placement programs at the local and state levels. The fragmented services we now provide should be replaced by a uniform system.

Employment And Training Boards

The leaders of our communities should take responsibility for building a comprehensive system that meets their needs. The local Employment and Training Boards for each major labor market would:

- Take responsibility for the school-to-work and Youth Center-to-work transition for young people, and for their further counseling on education, training and work opportunities.

- Manage and oversee the alternative certification system for school dropouts through the Youth Centers.

- Manage and oversee a second chance system for adults seeking the Certificate of Initial Mastery. This system would be operated in conjunction with the Youth Center program, but may require separate facilities and programs for adults.

- Manage and oversee the system for awarding Technical and Professional Certificates at the local level.

- Manage a labor market information system to guide program planning. The Board would maintain a data base containing detailed information on the offerings of service providers (including their quality record and the costs of their services). It would also include information concerning the number of trainees registered in all areas of training in any given year, the annual record of placements, job openings and the expected demand for labor in all fields.

- Manage a labor exchange service, which would provide information, counseling and contacts for individuals seeking job opportunities. The service would draw heavily on the data base just described.

- Coordinate existing programs concerned with job placement, vocational education, customized job training, JTPA and welfare related job training.

The Boards should be composed of company, union and public officials, as well as representatives of community based organizations. The Boards should also be able to compensate and attract a highly professional staff.

Service on the Board should be regarded as a mark of high honor and membership on the staff should be seen as a high

The local Employment and Training Boards for each major labor market would:

- *Take responsibility for the school-to-work and Youth Center-to-work transition for young people.*

- *Manage and oversee the Youth Centers.*

- *Manage and oversee a second chance system for adults seeking the Certificate of Initial Mastery.*

- *Manage and oversee the system for awarding Technical and Professional Certificates at the local level.*

- *Manage a labor market information system.*

- *Manage and oversee the job service.*

- *Coordinate existing programs.*

We envision a new, more comprehensive system where skills upgrading for the majority of our workers becomes a central aim of public policy. It begins with the initial skills preparation of youth and their school-to-work transition. It continues with the operation of skills upgrading programs for adult workers who have jobs, or are between jobs. It ties together this central mission with job information, employment counseling, job placement and income maintenance for the unemployed.

point in one's career. Boards can and should be designed to attract some of the most competent and dedicated people in the community.

In cases where labor, management and the community agree they have been effective, Private Industrial Councils could be used as a base on which to build the Boards.

The states would need to create a parallel structure to support the local boards, coordinate statewide functions and establish state standards for their operation.

States would also need to work with each other, perhaps through an interstate compact, and with the Federal government, to make the national system work smoothly.

As part of this national structure, it would be wise for the President to create a Cabinet council that would be directly responsible to the Office of the President for coordination of Federal government policy and programs relating to human resources policy.

A New Approach To American Labor Market Philosophy

Underlying this proposed structure is a philosophical change in the way we as a nation view human resources policies. Traditionally we have operated systems that work on the margins of our labor market, linked primarily to income maintenance

systems for the disadvantaged and dislocated workers, using short-term training as one means of assisting with job placement.

We envision a new, more comprehensive system where skills upgrading for the majority of our workers becomes a central aim of public policy. It begins with the initial skills preparation of youth and their school-to-work transition. It continues with the operation of skills upgrading programs for adult workers who have jobs, or are between jobs. It ties together this central mission with job information, employment counseling, job placement and income maintenance for the unemployed.

It is this bold, new agenda which necessitates the creation of a more uniform system to replace the existing variety of agencies.

14

IN CONCLUSION

America is headed toward an economic cliff. We will no longer be able to put a higher proportion of our people to work to generate economic growth. If basic changes are not made, real wages will continue to fall, especially for the majority who do not graduate from four-year colleges. The gap between economic 'haves' and 'have nots' will widen still further and social tensions will deepen.

Our recommendations provide an alternative for America. We do not pretend that this vision will be easily accepted or quickly implemented. But we also cannot pretend that the status quo is an option. It is no longer possible to be a high wage, low skill nation. We have choices to make:

- Do we continue to define educational success as 'time in the seat,' or choose a new system that focuses on the demonstrated achievement of high standards?

- Do we continue to provide little incentive for non-college students to study hard and take tough subjects, or choose a system that will reward real effort with better pay and better jobs?

- Do we continue to turn our backs on America's school dropouts, or choose to take responsibility for educating them?

- Do we continue to provide unskilled workers for unskilled jobs, or train skilled workers and give companies incentives to deploy them in high performance work organizations?

- Do we continue in most companies to limit training to a select handful of managers and professionals, or choose to provide training to front-line workers as well?

- Do we cling to a public employment and training system fragmented by institutional barriers, muddled by overlapping bureaucracies and operating at the margins of the labor market, or do we choose a unified system that addresses itself to a majority of workers?

- Do we continue to remain indifferent to the low wage path being chosen by many companies, or do we provide incentives for high productivity choices?

It is no longer possible to be a high wage, low skill nation. We have choices to make.

The system we propose
provides a uniquely American
solution. Boldly executed, it
has the potential not simply
to put us on an equal footing
with our competitors, but to
allow us to leap ahead, to
build the world's premier
workforce. In so doing, we
will create a formidable
competitive advantage.

Taken together, the Commission's recommendations provide the framework for developing a high quality American education and training system, closely linked to high performance work organizations. The system we propose provides a uniquely American solution. Boldly executed, it has the potential not simply to put us on an equal footing with our competitors, but to allow us to leap ahead, to build the world's premier workforce. In so doing, we will create a formidable competitive advantage.

The status quo is not an option. The choice we have is to become a nation of high skills or one of low wages.

The choice is ours. It should be clear. It must be made.

The
Study

THE STUDY

This Commission is deeply indebted to many who have studied the skills of America's workforce before us. Two recent reports stand out. *Workforce 2000: Work and Workers for the 21st Century*, produced by the Hudson Institute under a grant from the United States Department of Labor, made a powerful case for putting the issue of workers' skills squarely on the nation's agenda. *The Forgotten Half: Non-College Youth in America*, a report from the William T. Grant Commission on Work, Family and Citizenship, made an eloquent plea for attention to the needs of American youth who do not go to college. This is the group with which this Commission is primarily concerned. Together, these reports defined the starting point for our work.

The study which supports this report was carried out by a research team of 23 loaned executives from companies, unions, industry associations and the United States Department of Labor. The work began in July of 1989 and was completed in June of 1990.

Our study began in the United States, where we divided the American economy into industry groups and interviewed firms in each one.

Starting at the top of the firm, we asked the executives to define their market and their competitive environment, what the drivers of competitive success in their industry are, how they organize their workplaces, how their work organization is changing, what skills their workers need, what they are doing to make sure those skills are available and what government services they use. Then we went down to the shop floor, office or construction site and asked a different set of questions: How is each job defined? What skills are required to perform that job? How are people's assignments changing? Are managers having trouble hiring people with the needed skills, and, if so, what is being done about it?

When we had completed these interviews, we went abroad to six countries: Germany, Sweden, Denmark, Ireland, Japan and Singapore. There, we repeated the process on a somewhat attenuated scale, selecting and interviewing firms in a wide range of industries, asking much the same questions we had asked at home. We also conducted interviews and gathered data on the economic and human resources policies of those countries, as well as the structure and operation of their social programs, particularly those relating to education, training and other labor market policies. Here, too, we relied not just on publicly available data, but went further, interviewing people at every level of the system, from cabinet ministers to people taking courses in training centers. Gradually, we put together a composite picture, in some detail, of how the whole system fits together in each country, how values interact with policy, practice, history and demography to frame the way each nation is going about the business of developing a skilled workforce.

We concentrated the next stage of our research in several states. In each of these states, we selected one or two major labor markets. Just as we had done abroad, we proceeded to put together a picture of the labor market and how it actually operates, how federal, state and local policies interact with the practice of private firms, public agencies and education and training institutions to define the American system for skill development and employer demand for skilled labor.

We then drew upon the experience of a number of our Commissioners and Case Team members and asked them to prepare papers in selected fields of expertise. These included looks at the history of federal and state labor market policies; an analysis of apprenticeship and industry institute training

models; an analysis of 'best practice' programs for dropout recovery and public training; a view of educational assessment models now under study in various states; and a paper on the financing of America's labor and education systems.

Before we were done, we conducted interviews with more than 2,000 people at more than 550 firms and agencies, not counting innumerable local labor market interviews. All along, we read a small mountain of government and private reports and analyzed data not based on our own field research.

The study was comprehensive in scope. Our subject required the integration of information from diverse disciplines: corporate strategy, labor market policy and educational policy across a number of countries. While our work was thorough, it was conducted as a strategy study, not an academic inquiry. Our intent was to gather sufficient information and do adequate analysis to make policy recommendations.

Our conclusions are based in part upon data from our study. They are also based on the collective wisdom of our Commissioners, who have years of experience addressing issues of labor policy, education and corporate strategy.

Supporting Information

SUPPORTING INFORMATION I
A NEW AMERICAN ASSESSMENT SYSTEM FOR FOUNDATION SKILLS

Assessment System For Foundation Skills

Properly designed, an assessment system should function both to motivate and organize students' work during the school years and set a benchmark to which educational institutions could target their efforts. To meet these objectives, the system we recommend should:

- Reward effort and organized work.

- Demand thinking and reasoning skills of this nation's students, preparing them for more complex work environments.

- Directly assess thinking based achievement, using examinations equal to the task.

- Allow students to accumulate evidence of achievement and accomplishment, rather than relying on a single point of examination to determine performance.

- Be administered and directed by an independent certification agency.

Effort Based, Not Arbitrary, Education And Assessment

This Commission proposes an educational system that provides clear incentives and goals for students, measures educational attainment and skill competencies and rewards a student for effort and performance.

The current educational structure in the United States does not adequately measure nor reward a student's effort or academic performance. Due to the way they are examined and graded, students are not held to a clear standard of achievement toward which they can work.

For students who do not plan to go to college, high-school grades often have little meaning. As very few employers scrutinize high-school transcripts when making hiring decisions, what compels students to do more than the minimum required to obtain a passing grade? What motivates a student to work hard in school?

Grades have more meaning for college bound students, but grades alone do not determine a student's acceptance or rejection from the college of choice. Admissions officers look at performance on standardized national tests, like the ACT and the SAT. However, school curricula are not directly tied to these tests. Students have no way of adequately preparing for them, save the cram courses that teach shortcuts, but not subject content. Compounding this, teachers are often advised not to deliberately prepare their students for these exams so as to avoid being accused of giving them an 'unfair' advantage.

For either type of student, effort is not directly tied to results. Currently, no one can be held accountable for how students perform in school. If students who barely make it through the system receive the same reception in the workplace as those who really put forth an effort, is it surprising that some students do not take their education seriously?

An examination based achievement certification system can fundamentally change this. At the heart of such a system must be a series of examinations for which students can explicitly prepare, with teachers serving as their coaches, mentors and allies.

Thinking Based Achievement, Not Routinized Skills

Like other industrialized countries in the nineteenth century, the United States developed two different levels of educational expectation — one for an academic elite, the other, for the rest of the population. The majority of students was expected to learn routine skills, simple computation, reading of predictable texts and reciting civic or religious codes. They were not expected to learn higher-order functions of thinking and reasoning. These goals were reserved for the elite, originally in separate high schools and more recently in college preparatory programs in our comprehensive schools. The curriculum most Americans are exposed to gives them little chance to learn to construct convincing arguments and to understand complex systems.

A thinking oriented curriculum for all constitutes a significant new educational agenda. While it is not new to include thinking, problem solving and reasoning in some students' school curriculum, it is new to include it in everyone's curriculum. It is new to aspire seriously to make thinking and problem solving regular aspects of the school program for the entire population, including minorities, non-English speakers and children of the poor. To meet the challenge, we must have an achievement certification system in which the examinations assess the kinds of high level competencies to which we aspire. Current forms of testing do this very poorly.

The system of routinized rather than thinking based achievement forms the basis for testing theory and practice even today.

Multiple-choice tests reflect a 'Tayloristic' view of learning which is based on the proposition that knowledge and skills can be broken into discrete components.

Standardized tests used for secondary school students favor superficial answers not based on real understanding over those requiring thoughtful analysis. For example, reading sections require students to absorb a 300-word passage and then answer five to eight content-related questions in the space of six minutes. In math sections, students are faced with a string of unrelated math problems, which they must solve at a rate of about one per minute. As with all multiple-choice exams, the only way for a student to receive full points for an answer is to shade in the appropriate circle. There is no possibility for partial credit, even if the student's flow of logic was correct up until the last step in solving the problem.

As it exists, the testing system this country uses to measure its students discourages the development of higher order thinking. The result is that the system puts out people well-suited to the 'Tayloristic' work environments in which many will find themselves. But, as we have stressed, we see work organization heading in another direction, a direction that will necessitate adaptive learning on the job.

Direct Assessment: Performances, Portfolios, Projects

We need a different kind of examination to assess the abilities we view as necessary. Indicators of competence, tests that predict how well someone might do on a direct achievement assessment, cannot motivate an effort oriented educational system. Nor can 'grade level' standards help. Scoring at grade level on the kinds of educational tests American schools mostly use today means only that at least half of the people in your grade who took the same test scored worse than you did. The tests provide a distribution of scores so that students can be ranked in comparison with one another. But they do not establish a standard of competence. They say nothing about what a student knows or is able to do. If everyone scores at or above grade level, educators are accused of cheating or other forms of malpractice.

To establish an achievement certification system that can organize academic effort and communicate clearly to the public and to employers what students have accomplished, we need to determine what students ought to know and be able to do when they leave school and then arrange to directly examine students' command of that knowledge or skill.

Three kinds of examinations can be used:

Performance Examinations. The Olympics and the performing arts use this type of examination to determine an individual's qualifications. It is equally well-suited to assess academic ability and effort. This exam differs fundamentally from the multiple-choice kind of test, in that it measures process as well as end product, and it has no elements of surprise. Students taking these exams are aware of the type of performance expected of them, and they are able to take the necessary steps in preparation. Teachers can prepare students for the exams, acting as coaches and mentors, rather than adversaries. In the system we envision, both traditional academic and more practical performance would be assessed. For example, practical literacy might be assessed by asking Certificate candidates to assemble equipment following written instructions and diagrams; and ability to work with others in making decisions might be assessed by rating candidates' performance in an economic simulation game.

Performance examinations could be carried out either in a live setting, with a team of judges grading specific features of the performance and the overall quality, or the product of the performance could be scored in place of the live performance. The latter option substantially reduces the cost of performance examination, making it a viable component of a mass assessment system.

Portfolio Examinations. This form of examination is modeled on methods of assessment used in the visual arts in which a team of judges rates students' products on several different criteria. Certain academic skills, especially writing, are well-suited to this type of assessment, as time based exams impose unnatural constraints and do not accurately capture a student's true ability. Current experiments show that this type of test can have direct educational value: by working with their teachers in selecting the best of their work for inclusion in the portfolio, students build explicit understanding of standards of judgment.

Project Examinations. The third form of examination evaluates extended participation in learning. These examinations are the best way of assessing motivation and social skills, because judges evaluate a record of candidates' extended participation in a task with real meaning and consequence in the world. For example, students might undertake an extended applied science project such as designing a bridge, conducting an investigation of an aspect of community life, or planning and carrying out a construction project. Students would be required to document the major steps taken, supervisors would sign off and rate the project at designated stages and a final grade would be determined, taking into account a whole range of criteria.

Any of these examinations taken alone would serve to provide a clear link between effort and assessment, measurable by the student, the teacher and the community at large. A combination of the exams, depending upon the skills or knowledge to be measured, would provide an even better picture of a student's achievement.

A Cumulative Certification System

These examinations should be viewed as building blocks rather than high stakes moments of possible failure. The achievement certification system we propose should permit students to assemble certification credentials over a period of years, perhaps beginning as early as entrance into middle school. This kind of cumulative certification has several advantages over a single point of examination.

- It helps to organize and motivate students over a period of years. Rather than preparing for a distant examination whose form and demands can be only dimly imagined by the 11- or 12-year-old, students can begin to collect specific certifications.

- It provides multiple opportunities for success. Cumulative certificates are our best shot at drawing in the presently undereducated and undermotivated.

- A cumulative credentialing system, because of its transferable nature, permits students who are not being well taught in the mainstream educational system to earn their credentials under other institutional auspices.

- This system avoids the problem of minimum credentialing standards becoming functionally the maximum. Students who complete the base certifications early in their schooling can start working on advanced certificates — either in schools and colleges or in workplace training sites.

- A cumulative system will avoid the phenomenon of 'examination hell' — a year or two of high-tension devotion to nothing but exam study — that plagues several countries (such as Japan and France) that have single point-of-exit examinations.

An Independent Examining Organization

Credentials and certification should be determined by an organization independent of school systems and free from political influence. The Governing Board of this organization should be broadly representative of educators, employers and the citizenry at large. Under the Board's general oversight, working commissions in several knowledge and skill domains should determine appropriate skills and knowledge for certification standards, establish the performance, portfolio and project examinations procedures and oversee the professional and objective nature of the judging of these exams.

SUPPORTING INFORMATION II
ALTERNATIVE PROGRAMS FOR AT-RISK YOUTH: SWEETWATER UNION HIGH SCHOOL, THE BOSTON COMPACT AND THE WEGMAN'S PROGRAM

The dropout problem and the ill-defined and often restrictive school-to-work transition have spurred communities from coast to coast to devise alternative programs for their youth. Sweetwater Union High School, the Boston Compact and the Wegman's Program are three good examples.

Sweetwater Union High School: Dropout Recovery

Three years ago, in a determined attempt to reduce its growing dropout rate, the Sweetwater Union High School District in San Diego, California set up an alternative system for students to acquire their high-school diplomas. Two relocatable buildings were set up next to the high school and equipped with classrooms of computers and software necessary to provide a full high-school course offering.

Sweetwater's superintendent found a way to reverse the traditional incentives that encourage professionals to get rid of the least desirable students. He decided to operate the program as a business. Ninety-four percent of the revenue (derived from the entire state allotment for each dropout attracted to the center) would go to the school. The school would pay all operating expenses including staff salaries, but the remaining 'profits' would belong to the school and could be spent at the principal's discretion.

Today, former dropouts sit at computer terminals, fully engaged in their studies, well-behaved and full of hope. Many are well on their way to receiving their diplomas. Of the most recent group of graduates, approximately 60 percent have enrolled in college. These are the very same students who, a few years earlier, would have been ejected from classrooms for disruptive behavior or who would have quietly slipped out of school, feeling it had nothing to offer.

The district does no recruiting for the program. Word of mouth has produced a waiting list of those who want to enroll.

The high quality of education the students receive and the flexibility of scheduling are key components of the success of the system. Students can both go to school and work full-time, and can participate in any of the school's extracurricular or social activities.

In a conventional program, the district would have had to build a $35 million physical facility for these students. But the relocatable classrooms and computer equipment cost a tiny fraction of that amount, and the program has required no new staff. Most important, 6,000 young people who had little to look forward to in life now have a good start.

The Boston Compact And Its Commitment To Boston's Youth

The current labor market structure makes it very difficult for low-income young people — White, Black or Hispanic — to get matched to jobs. The first roadblock they encounter is access to information or people concerning jobs. Too often, they and their parents lack the personal contacts and the resources of their middle class counterparts that would enable them to get that first interview.

The powerful negative stereotypes that exist on both sides of the hiring equation make looking for a job that much more difficult for these youth. Employers cannot help but be swayed by what they see in print about inner-city youth. And inner-city youth, especially minorities, have their own negative ideas about downtown hiring practices.

The Boston Compact, a community-wide commitment to improving the educational achievement of Boston's public school students, has put the issue on the city's agenda. Some of the strongest initiatives include:

- A school system commitment to measurable improvements in student attendance and academic achievement.

- A private sector commitment to employ students in the summer and upon graduation through the Boston Private Industry Council.

- The school-based Careers Service, which combines the resources of the school and business communities to create linkages between inner-city youth and employers.

- The contribution of $17 million by the business community to a fund to aid public education, including a 'last dollar scholarship' program for all graduates admitted to college.

- The agreement between city high schools and the 24 area colleges and universities to increase the number of students going to college and graduating.

- The commitment of the Area Building Trades Council (AFL-CIO) to increase the enrollment in apprenticeships for Boston high school graduates.

- A commitment to measure results carefully, including a survey of all students in the fall after graduation to ascertain their education and employment circumstances.

An examination of one of the programs, the Careers Service, shows how commitment to youth can ease the school-to-work transition, especially for the disadvantaged.

The Service, a joint effort of Boston's educational and business communities, under the direction of Boston's Private Industry Council, employs career specialists who work with students, teachers, staff and employers to pair students with jobs. There are no guarantees for employment. Both the students and the employers must be convinced that the matches fit before any commitments are made on either side.

Currently, some 900 firms in the city participate in the summer jobs and the graduate hire programs. Personnel officers work with the service's career specialists, exchanging information and opening doors that were formerly closed to students.

The results have been dramatic. In 1989, 3,316 high-school students found summer employment at an average wage of $6.08 an hour. That same year, 1,107 graduates were hired for permanent, full-time positions at an average wage of $6.75 an hour. Graduates from Boston high schools found full-time jobs through the Careers Service, at an average wage of $8.43 an hour.

A comparison of the 1985 survey of Boston graduates with BLS numbers for the nation shows employment for 62 percent of the White (10 points above the national rate), 60 percent of the Black (32 points above), and more than half the Hispanic graduates (11 points better than the national rate).

Employment/Population Ratios for Class of 1985

	U.S.A.	Boston
Whites	52%	62%
Hispanics	43%	54%
Blacks	28%	60%

For graduates of the class of 1988, the Boston PIC reported that 66 percent of Whites, 58 percent of Blacks and 71 percent of Hispanics were employed.

An analysis of wages a year and a half after graduation for the class of 1988 by Professor Andrew Sum of Northeastern's Center for Labor Market Studies shows Boston's non-college youth earning $8.04 an hour, nearly half again as much as the $5.40 non-college high-school graduates in other central cities surveyed by the Census Bureau.

This survey's results are important in two ways: First, they show how much a commitment to improving current systems can provide students, regardless of background, with a positive future; second, they underline the need for accessibility and timely transmittal of data so that those involved can see the concrete results of their hard work and effort.

While the external partners have made progress toward their goals, school improvement has come slowly in Boston. At the Boston PIC annual meeting in 1988, the business community and the mayor refused to renew the Compact until satisfied that the structure of the schools would improve. By March, 1989, when Compact II was at last signed, the leadership of the Boston Public Schools and the Boston Teachers Union had committed to a contract incorporating school based management and a new accountability system that measures individual school performance.

Recognizing that entry level jobs are not enough to assure economic security, Compact II sets a goal of building links between work and further learning during the four years after high school for those students not going to college. The first project under this new effort is designed to lead to professional certification and an associate's degree in the health professions for students.

With technical assistance from the National Alliance of Business, 12 cities in addition to Boston are developing compacts based on agreements between schools, business and government to carefully measure progress toward improvement in education and employment for young people.

The Wegman's Program

Wegman's Supermarkets in Rochester, New York offers an example of a company that has taken up the challenge on its own. For several years, the owners of Wegman's have been offering part-time supermarket jobs to 14-year-old students who are identified by the local schools as likely potential dropouts. The one condition for employment is that the students must stay in school to keep the job.

A Wegman's employee works at the school district headquarters to coordinate the program with parents and teachers, recruit students, monitor their progress and help them out if they get in trouble. Employees at the supermarkets act as mentors for the students on the job and also tutor them in their school subjects. Best of all, for any student who succeeds in finishing school and continues onto college, Wegman's pays the full tuition. The result is that Wegman's has single-handedly managed to create a multifaceted and caring support structure for the students that hinges upon the students' continuing effort to learn.

SUPPORTING INFORMATION III
AMERICAN EXAMPLES OF SUCCESSFUL WORKER TRAINING

There is no single recipe for successful worker training. Some of the most exemplary programs in the nation differ greatly in approach, administration and scope. Some successful experiments are being initiated by unions in cooperation with employers and educational institutions and by high schools and community colleges working together.

Industry Network Training
The Sheet Metal Industry — Training The Skilled Craftsmen

High geographic mobility characterizes the sheet metal industry. A worker in Jackson, Mississippi on Monday could find himself working in San Francisco, California on Friday of the same week. He and his employer would not expect the difference in locale to have any bearing on his ability to work. Formerly, it did. Due to the wide diversity in content and quality of training practices around the country, there was no guarantee of consistency in work habits.

Recognizing this, the union and the employers' association, through a nationwide Collective Bargaining Agreement, created a National Training Trust Fund in 1971 to research current training practices. The Fund looked to sheet metal workers and employers throughout the country for ideas. From their responses and suggestions, the Fund devised a national apprentice training curriculum and a loan/grant program for equipment and facility upgrade. (The program made monies available in interest-free long-term loans and outright grants.)

The study also unveiled some serious shortcomings in the existing system. For the most part, industry practice was to offer a one-time program for apprentices only. The need for continuing education and skills upgrading of journeymen went largely ignored. In 1973, the Training Fund, in conjunction with the National Center for Research in Vocational Education at Ohio State University, devised a 'train-the-trainer' program to raise the teaching ability of local instructors and to introduce them to the concept of continuous training, for apprentices through master craftsmen.

Since the start of this program 16 years ago, more than 3,000 instructors have been trained, and many local sheet metal Joint

Apprenticeship and Training Committees (JATC's) now offer training beyond the apprenticeship level. Programs include welding, computer-assisted design (CAD) and computer-assisted manufacturing (CAM), indoor air quality, architectural sheet metal and other advanced studies.

The Fund continues to closely monitor employment requirements and forecasts skill needs for the industry's future. Growing concerns about energy conservation have prompted a training program for energy management technicians and auditors. Technicians are trained to examine the energy efficiency of existing buildings. Following the program, they have the skills to retrofit structures to improve energy efficiency and indoor air quality.

National network training programs modeled around similar principles now exist for six other building trades.

Joint Apprenticeship/Degree Programs

Skilled trades in other industries are taking another approach to training. They are structuring apprenticeship programs to allow apprentices to apply coursework and experience toward the attainment of an associate's degree.

The National Joint Apprenticeship and Training Committee for Operating Engineers, the American Association of Community and Junior Colleges (AACJC) and the American Council on Education (ACE) are working on this dual enrollment model. The joint management and union committee has reached agreement upon a general structure and curriculum (including content and instructional material) for the apprenticeships, subject to some local variation. Local administrators are encouraged to concentrate on more macro issues rather than be delayed or limited by rigid specifications. The AACJC provides technical support in course planning and implementation.

Colleges have been granting apprentices in these dual enrollment programs credits equivalent to 50 to 80 percent of the total credits needed for an associate's degree.

Joint Union/Employer Training
United Automobile Workers And The Auto Industry

Since the early 1980's, the United Automobile Workers (UAW) has successfully negotiated dedicated training funds into its contracts with major auto companies.

Ford Motor Company. The National Education, Development and Training Center (NEDTC), located on the campus of Henry Ford Community College, to this point has provided training for about half of Ford's hourly workforce.

While much of the training in technical literacy, problem solving and teamwork for UAW-represented Ford employees takes place after working hours, a great deal of it is clearly linked to the training sponsored on company time. As the company has emphasized statistical process control training for its workers, the NEDTC has provided courses in remedial math and computer awareness for those who need to acquire basic skills. More than 30,000 workers have participated in this companion training.

Since the UAW and Ford decided to make training a strategic issue, the company's financial profile has moved from losses to profits. The 1988 annual report noted: "Ford learned a pivotal lesson during the bleak days of the early 1980's — if the company was to be successful it had to focus on the basics of its business and engage the full support of its employees." Ford recognizes NEDTC as having played an integral role in this turnaround.

General Motors. Every one of the 157 General Motors facilities in the United States has UAW training programs in place. AC Rochester is among the most active.

AC Rochester has undergone tremendous change in a short period of time. In 1985, AC Rochester produced carburetors. Since then, the plant has introduced a new production process and technology, and now the primary product is fuel injection systems.

Organizational changes have followed in the wake. The previous 112 production classifications have been collapsed into three. Because of this dramatic restructuring, employees (25 percent of whom do not possess a high-school education) have to be retrained, their skills upgraded and their versatility increased. Job-specific training is mandatory and is offered to workers on a seniority basis. If workers experience difficulty completing required job skill training, alternative basic skills coursework is provided for them. Workers are allowed to repeat a training course, if necessary, until needed job skill competencies are obtained.

AC Rochester pays for this training using both UAW-GM funds and public resources. Approximately 20 percent of AC Rochester's employees are enrolled in at least one of the program's 75 job-specific training modules.

GED education programs (started in 1986), Adult Basic Education and English as a Second Language programs supplement job-specific training for approximately 680 AC Rochester workers. New York State's Employer Specific Skills Training Grant and Workplace Literacy funds provide training for another 30 percent of the plant's workers.

Seven hundred and fifty workers are in the plant's JOBS bank, a job security program created in the UAW-GM national agreement. All JOBS bank workers, as well as all active workers in the plant, can take part in a full-time college attendance program created by AC Rochester's joint training center staff. Upon completion of a GED/Workplace Literacy Program, an active worker or a JOBS bank worker is eligible to enter the full-time college program. Both active and JOBS bank workers receive full pay and benefits, plus up to $2,250 annual tuition payments while enrolled in the college program. To remain eligible, workers must obtain a minimum of 15 credit hours per semester and be matriculated into an associate's, bachelor's or master's degree granting program. Approximately 50 percent of the workers in training at AC Rochester are enrolled in the full-time college attendance program.

Chrysler. The UAW-Chrysler National Training Center, headquartered near downtown Detroit, operates eight United States regional training centers near major Chrysler plant locations and directs 45 different training and joint activity programs in 41 locations in the United States.

More than 60 percent of UAW-represented Chrysler workers participate in some kind of formal training or educational program, ranging from 'Tech Prep' basic skill development to new technology training. (More than 30,000 UAW-represented Chrysler workers have participated in computer training alone.) The National Training Center has experimented with a number of new training and educational techniques and has undertaken a number of special pilot programs in 'Tech Prep' training.

'Two-Plus-Two' Programs In Technical Fields

A growing number of communities are creating better linkages between high schools and community colleges. Experimental 'two-plus-two' programs can be found across the country, creating a bridge for students who do not pursue four-year college degrees.

A 'Tech Prep' program in North Carolina's Richmond County School District is an example of this link. Prior to the establishment of the program, 25 percent of the district's high-school students were enrolled in college preparatory courses, and the remaining 75 percent in general academic/vocational courses. For three quarters of the student body, courses were outdated and did not reflect the needs of the community.

In 1986, the district decided that the vocational track needed attention. A 'Tech Prep' program was created with upgraded and revised vocational courses. These courses reflected the demands of Richmond employers, and they required more rigorous academic and vocational preparation than traditional non-college programs of study.

The program has been most successful. Today, about one third of Richmond's students are enrolled in college preparatory programs and another third can be found in the 'Tech Prep' program. Enrollment for Algebra I courses has increased by 42 percent, and Algebra II course enrollment has gone up by 57 percent in just three years. Mathematics has not been the only area affected by the system's reform. More students are taking advanced English, social studies and science courses, and the average SAT scores for the district have increased 46 points. Additionally, the annual dropout rate has declined from 7.2 percent to 4.8 percent. The number of graduates choosing to attend community college has doubled.

SUPPORTING INFORMATION IV:
SKILLS INVESTMENT TAXES: FOREIGN EXAMPLES

All of the foreign competitors we studied require firms to invest in developing and improving the skills of their workers. These contributions, organized as part of national strategies for training and skills development, generally take two forms.

Companies often directly contribute to public employment and training services, as in Germany, Japan and Denmark. Through this approach, the government may organize, oversee or directly provide the training to those individuals needing basic or upgraded work skills.

Firms are often required to contribute through a periodically assessed tax or levy to a national training fund, as in Ireland, Singapore and Sweden. This fund may operate as a monitored 'training account,' from which companies can retrieve their funds to offer some form of approved training.

The funds for these initiatives are channeled from various sources such as payroll taxes, general government revenue and tax-deductible contributions, all of which are expenditures above and beyond a company's in-house training investment. In every case, the goal of the national system is to encourage companies to train, to spread costs and ultimately to create a self-perpetuating program for continually upgrading the skills of the adult workforce.

GERMANY

German corporations contribute a total of nearly 3.5 percent of annual payroll to public training and employment schemes through joint employer-employee financed national unemployment insurance, the national system of apprenticeship and mandatory contributions to local Chambers of Commerce.

In this system, employers are assessed 2.3 percent of annual payroll to the unemployment insurance fund, and employees match their contributions. In 1988, 42 percent of this fund was devoted to training and labor exchange programs, including employment counseling and placement, incentives for companies to employ and retrain hard-to-place workers and free training for workers who are unemployed or facing unemployment for skills reasons. Although this fund is managed by the government, the training is provided by the private sector and generally lasts from four months to two years. Individuals receive the normal unemployment benefit to support themselves during training.

Beyond this expense, German companies contribute DM 25 billion (U.S. $13.5 billion), or another 2.5 percent of payroll, for 1.7 million trainees in the apprenticeship system. Through these apprenticeships, companies largely finance the last two to four years of secondary education for the majority of German youth.

In addition to the contributions to apprenticeships and insurance fund programs, German companies are required to contribute to their local employers' organizations (generally the Chambers of Industry and Commerce or the Crafts Chambers). Seventy percent of the Chamber budgets are devoted to training purposes, geared particularly to those small companies that lack the resources to train extensively in-house.

Many larger German corporations, along with funding public training, dedicate significant resources to their own training initiatives. For example, Seimens AG allocated DM 470 million, or 2.5 percent of payroll, to train and upgrade its workers in-house in 1987.

SWEDEN

Swedish firms contribute to training by financing the public employment and training systems and by contributing to govern-ment-established training funds. An employer contribution of approximately 2.5 percent of annual payroll finances the National Labor Market Board (AMS), which operates Sweden's national employment service, manages labor exchange and provides training and subsidized employment. This contribution is independent of the unemployment compensation system, to which companies also contribute, and of the employer's extensive social security obligations. In 1987, Sweden spent $3.9 billion on labor market measures for a workforce of 4.4 million.

The Swedish government also establishes renewal funds, into which all companies of a certain size are required to contribute 10 percent of net profits. The tax-deductible contributions are placed into an interest-free account and may be withdrawn later to support company training that has been approved by the government and the local unions. Volvo, for example, utilized its renewal funds to provide up to two years of initial training for employees when it opened its team-style auto production plant in Udevalla.

DENMARK

In Denmark, training for unemployed individuals and a substantial amount of training for company employees is provided free of charge by the government through the National Labor Market Board (AMU). While general government revenues fund most of this effort, employers contribute up to 600 Dkr (U.S. $82) per worker. This figure represents a total employer contribution of 0.2 percent of annual payroll. Employees also match the contribution. In 1988, AMU provided 1.1 billion Dkr (U.S. $137 million) to train 100,000 participants.

IRELAND

In Ireland, the larger companies are required to contribute one to 2.5 percent of payroll annually into the levy-grant scheme, creating a fund similar to Sweden's renewal fund. Ninety percent of funds are then returned to the company for use in training programs approved by the national employment authority (FAS). The remaining 10 percent is used for administrative purposes. FAS, working through its industrial training committees, assists companies in devising their training programs and administers the labor exchange system.

SINGAPORE

Singapore has aggressively supported training as part of its overall high productivity development strategy. The Skills Development Fund (SDF), to which employers contribute one percent of payroll annually, is used by the government to partially reimburse companies for approved forms of training. This includes approved apprenticeship and in-house training, external training in recognized courses offered by accredited institutions and particularly training in high technology and 'economically critical' skills (for which companies receive twice the normal reimbursement).

The Singapore government also funds from general revenues a number of training institutes, often in cooperation with multinational companies.

JAPAN

Japanese corporations have a strong philosophical commitment to training, and in many cases build and run their own schools and training centers for the constant betterment of their workforce.

Japanese corporations are required to contribute an average of one percent of payroll into the National Employment Insurance Fund, which pays for unemployment compensation and three employment and training programs. Of this one percent tax, about one third to one half is used to finance the three employment and training initiatives.

In addition, employer tax funds are combined with federal, prefectural (state) and, to a lesser degree, municipal general revenues to finance the Ministry of Labor's Human Resources Development Bureau, which administers the Capability Development Program. This program supports nearly 400 public or vocational training facilities, provides direct assistance to firms in creating their own in-house training capability and helps develop and implement a set of industry based skill certifications and examinations.

Each of these countries requires companies to promote the skills development of the national workforce. In each case, the mandatory corporate contributions are in addition to the amounts that companies spend to train their own employees.

SUPPORTING INFORMATION V
FINANCING OUR PROPOSALS

The United States spends more than $300 billion each year in Federal, state and local funds on public and private education at all levels. This Commission's recommendations constitute a system of quality controls to assure we are getting the most for these dollars.

What The Current System Costs

Before estimating the costs of these recommendations, the Commission estimated the amount of public funds currently being spent on the 16- to 19-year-old population. These monies include the last two years of high school, two years of college, government-sponsored training programs like the Job Training Partnership Act and employment assistance like the Targeted Jobs Tax Credit and Unemployment Insurance.

Using 1987-1988 data (the last school year with the most comprehensive enrollment and revenue information available), we estimate that between $34.2 and $36.5 billion of public funds were spent on the operating expenses of education and training programs and for employment assistance for civilians in this age group.

The Focus Population

Age	Total Population	Post-Secondary Enrollment	Grades 11-12 Enrollment
16-19	14,548,500	2,903,737	5,795,822

Public Expenditures:
Education Operating Costs And Training-Related Programs

For The 16- To 19-Year-Old Population		*Public Expenditures* *($ Billions)*
Secondary School:		**$23.1 - 24.7**[1]
Grade 11	11.7 - 12.5	
Grade 12	10.7 - 11.4	
Unclassified	0.7 - 0.8	
Higher Education:		**7.8 - 8.5**[2]
Public Institutions	7.4 - 7.9	
Federal	0.3 - 0.4	
State	6.2 - 6.3	
Local	0.5 - 0.6	
Pell Grants	0.4 - 0.6	
Private Institutions	0.4 - 0.6	
Federal	0.1 - 0.1	
State	0.1 - 0.2	
Local	< 0.1	
Pell Grants	0.2 - 0.3	

Employment and/or Training Assistance:[3]

JTPA Programs	**2.2**
(including Block Grants, Summer Youth Program, Dislocated Workers, Job Corps, Native Americans and Migrant Worker programs, JTPA for Veterans)	
Employment Service	**0.2**
Unemployment Insurance	**0.3**
Other Second Chance Programs	**0.4**
(including Vocational Rehabilitation, Food Stamp Employment & Training, WIN/JOBS, Refugee Assistance)	
Targeted Jobs Tax Credit	**< 0.1**

TOTAL	**$34.2 - 36.5**

In calculating these costs, the Commission counted only those public funds associated with current fund operating expenses for 16- to 19-year-olds. Capital outlays, interest on debt, research money, and both restricted and unrestricted grants and contracts were excluded.[4]

As the above charts indicate, the bulk of public cost is attributable to state and local funds for junior and senior years of public high school and to state expenditures for the two years of public higher education immediately following high school.

Youth Centers

Bringing disenfranchised groups into an education system, any system — be it public high school, Job Corps or new Youth Centers — will require additional funds.

In calculating a cost, the Commission made several assumptions. First, the Youth Center participants may have special needs that result in higher than average per pupil expenses. Thus, we increased by 20 percent the 1988 per pupil average for grades K-12 to arrive at a Youth Center per pupil expenditure of just under $5,100.

Second, because the majority of dropouts leave school at age 16 or 17, we assumed that the average length of enrollment in a Youth Center would be two years. Once a person has attained the Certificate of Initial Mastery, the individual would pursue

the various options available through work or more advanced technical and professional training.

Age	1989 Population[5]	Dropout Rate	Annual Youth Center Costs[6] (in billions)
16	3,351,000	20%	3.4
17	3,534,000	20%	3.6
18	3,676,000	20%	3.7
19	3,662,000	20%	3.7

To date, attempts at solving our nation's dropout problem have been expensive, frustrating and largely unsuccessful. Our continued failure means greater costs for society:

- Fifty-two percent of high-school dropouts are unemployed or receiving welfare assistance. For this population of Americans, welfare benefits and lost tax revenues totaled $75 billion in 1987.[7]

- More than 80 percent of pregnant teenagers are high-school dropouts.[8]

- Sixty percent of prison inmates are high-school dropouts. The annual cost to house an individual in prison is more than $16,000.[9]

The Commission believes that while the sums of money it proposes for Youth Centers are not small, the costs are minimal compared with the incalculable benefits to be derived from a total population of 'work-ready' individuals. The proposed system makes it very difficult for individuals to slip through the cracks — meaning that nearly 100 percent of our young people should acquire the basic mastery skills necessary to lead productive work lives.

Funding Technical and Professional Certificates

If we had paid up to $5,000 for every 16-, 17-, 18- and 19-year-old to pursue education beyond the Certificate of Initial Mastery in 1987-1988, the cost would have amounted to $72.7 billion (versus roughly $36.5 billion spent under the current system).

The Commission has suggested that the National Center on Education and the Economy conduct a detailed analysis of this subject and explore ways to ensure that all students have the financial means to pursue this further education.

Given the anticipated economic benefits to society, a strong argument can be made that general revenues should be used to finance this type of guarantee. The original G.I. Bill is one example of how an initial government investment can produce measurable benefits for many years. At a cost of about $14 billion, the G.I. Bill provided training and education for more than 7.8 million World War II veterans. A recent congressional study concluded that, of those who used the entitlement to attend college, the ratio of benefits to costs was a minimum of 5 to 1 and as high as 12.5 to 1. The study also found that the additional taxes paid by the college educated veterans during their working lives more than paid for the program.[10]

Another example of a high ratio of benefits to costs is found in quality preschool programs, such as Head Start. These programs demonstrate that for every federal dollar spent, $3 to $6 is saved in future social services, welfare, unemployment and remediation.[11]

Other funding strategies could be used to make the proposal 'revenue-neutral.'

Individual Training Account: Individual Training Accounts (ITAs) could be established that would combine a voucher system similar to the G.I. Bill with a savings and equity based financing system analogous to Individual Retirement Accounts (IRAs).[12] Students would make tax-deductible contributions and withdrawals to purchase training and education. Most importantly, negative account balances would be permitted while an individual is enrolled in an education or training program; repayments to the account would begin once the individual began working and would be spread over time.

Training Surcharge on Personal Income:

A plan similar to the Individual Training Account could permit an individual to repay a four-year government-backed education and training voucher over the course of one's working life. Payments would take the form of a small surcharge (less than one percent of personal income) on one's annual tax return.

Both the Individual Training Account and the Training Surcharge would allow young people to purchase education and training when they need it and repay the debt later. Also, both plans could be used throughout one's lifetime as an incentive for further training. Employers as well as employees could make contributions to an Individual Training Account.

Skills Development Fund

The Skills Development Fund will be financed through the federal training trust fund. This trust will not require any General Fund expenditures since it will be created with revenues collected from the assessment on every employer who chooses not to invest in employee training. One percent of the current United States payroll would produce between $28 and $30 billion annually. Because a small percentage of companies already spend one percent or more on training and more can be expected to do the same as a direct result of the assessment, the trust fund will total less than this amount in the first year.

Other Proposals

We recognize that our other recommendations have fiscal implications, including those related to Technical and Professional Certification, Employment and Training Boards and the Certificate of Initial Mastery. But, in relation to the costs just described, the amounts are small and likely to be supported by reallocating currently available resources and drawing on the resources of the private sector.

An example of how the Technical and Professional Certification system can operate is the Advisory Committee for Trade Negotiations and its network of smaller industry specific groups.

In the Trade Act of 1974, Congress established a private sector advisory committee system to ensure that trade policy reflected United States commercial and economic interests. The system consists of approximately 40 committees with a total membership of approximately 1,000 advisors, who serve on policy, technical, sectoral and functional advisory committees. Each advisor represents a different industry or commodity group.

All advisors, who are nominated by their peers, serve a finite term without compensation for their time or expenses. With the exception of the initial selection process and the staff support of a few government employees, there is no other federal role and no budget outlay. The committees meet regularly, are self-governed and are considered prestigious and effective.

NOTES:

1. 1987-1988 public school enrollment for grade 11 was 2,935,615; 1987-1988 public school enrollment for grade 12 was 2,680,843. Using the official 1987 and 1988 per pupil current expenditure averages for grades K through 12 of $3,977 and $4,243 respectively (based upon average daily attendance) one can calculate a range of $23.1-$24.7 billion of total spending for grades 11 and 12. The Commission notes that per pupil expenses for secondary school are greater than those for the elementary grades (due to the costs of senior high school laboratories, vocational programs and smaller class sizes). In addition, some private secondary schools receive revenues from Federal, state and local government sources; however these amounts are minimal and data are not available. Because the published data do not satisfactorily measure the size or place of enrollment, the Commission assumed that most individuals benefiting from public vocational monies would be counted in high school or in two-year community college programs.

   Source: National Center for Education Statistics; "Digest of Education Statistics - 1989."

2. The Commission counted all 18- and 19-year-olds enrolled in all institutions of higher learning. In 1987-1988 this number was 2,696,652 or 21.1 percent of total post- secondary enrollment. (Those individuals younger than age 18 who were enrolled in these institutions totaled 207,085 or about 1.6 percent of all higher education students.)

The Commission applied all federal, state and local appropriations, including Pell Grants, to the proportion of enrolled 18- and 19-year-olds (by public, private, four-year and two-year institutions) to produce a range of $7.8-$8.5 billion.

Source: National Center for Education Statistics; "Digest of Education Statistics - 1989."

3. The Commission used the United States Departments of Labor, Agriculture, Treasury and Health and Human Services estimates of the proportion of 16- to 19-year-olds being served by government programs. These proportions were then applied to total program budgets.

4. By counting only government appropriations for current student expenditures, the Commission realized it was losing some federal, state and local funds that ultimately do contribute to student instruction, such as state incentive grants to students and local scholarships. Due to the lack of detailed data, the Commission chose to underestimate rather than overestimate the figures.

5. 1989 unpublished data from the current population survey, the Bureau of Labor Statistics, United States Department of Labor.

6. The Commission used the United States average dropout rate (as officially defined) of 20 percent to calculate the anticipated costs of the Youth Centers. The high-school graduation rate is another measure that can be used. In 1989, the nation's high schools graduated about 71 percent of those students who entered secondary school, according to the United States Department of Education. Based on this rate, the cost of educating 29 percent of today's 16-year-old population in Youth Centers (with an annual per pupil expenditure of $5,100) would be about $4.9 billion per year or $9.8 billion for two years.

7. Data from research conducted by the Multicultural Prevention Resources Center, San Francisco and published as an article "A Nation in Crisis: The Dropout Dilemma," by Byron N. Kunisawa in *NEA Today*, January 1988.

8. Ibid.

9. 1988 data from the National Institute of Corrections Information Center, Boulder, Colorado.

10. "A Cost-Benefit Analysis of Government Investment in Post Secondary Education under the World War II G.I. Bill," a staff analysis prepared for the use of the Subcommittee on Education and Health of the Joint Economic Committee. December 14, 1988.

11. "The Preschool Challenge" by Lawrence J. Schweinhart; High/Scope Educational Research Foundation. 1985.

    "Changed lives: The effects of the Perry Preschool program on youths through age 19," Monographs of the High/Scope Educational Research Foundation, by John R. Berrueta-Clement, Lawrence J. Schweinhart, W. Steven Barnett, Ann S. Epstein & David P. Weikart. 1984.

12. This concept is discussed in *The High Flex Society* by Pat Choate and J.K. Linger. 1986.

Acknowledgements

ACKNOWLEDGEMENTS

We thank Marc Tucker for the vision he displayed in defining the agenda on which this Commission has worked and the Board of Trustees of the National Center on Education and the Economy for providing us the opportunity to address that agenda.

We acknowledge with gratitude the financial support extended to the project by the Carnegie Corporation of New York, the State of New York, Towers Perrin, Cresap/ Telesis, SJS, Inc. and The German Marshall Fund of the United States which made the entire effort possible. None of these organizations is responsible for the statements or views expressed in this report.

We thank Joan Wills, the Project Manager, who shepherded the meetings of the Commission and staff and drew together the strings of what became an unusually wide ranging enterprise with admirable skill and tenacity.

Thanks are due, too, to the many organizations that contributed their executives to the Case Team research effort during an eight-month period and supported their expenses when in the field. Without their aid, it would have been impossible to mount the research program, which in many ways has given this Commission its distinctive character.

And, we owe our thanks, of course, to the case study research team members themselves, whose prodigious effort on three continents provided a unique perspective. Though technically on leave from their sponsoring institutions for part of this period, virtually all found that they simply had to add these time-consuming tasks to a full-time job, which they did without complaint and with great dedication.

The staffs of the National Center, Cresap/Telesis and SJS, Inc. provided support beyond the usual call of duty without complaint and with a high degree of professional skill, for which we are extremely grateful.

We would also like to express our appreciation to the thousands of people in the United States and abroad who allowed us to come and talk with them in the course of our research. Their hospitality and openness made it possible to form a picture of a very complex reality that could have been developed in no other way.

Commission on the Skills of the American Workforce

Appendices

COMMISSION ON THE SKILLS OF THE AMERICAN WORKFORCE
BIOGRAPHICAL SKETCHES

Ira C. Magaziner, *Chair*

Ira C. Magaziner is currently President of SJS, Inc., a consulting firm providing assistance to groups addressing economic and social issues facing America in the 1990's. Previously, he was Founder and President of Telesis, an international consulting firm specializing in corporate strategy and economic development policy. Mr. Magaziner continues to be a consulting associate with Telesis. Prior to founding Telesis in 1979, Mr. Magaziner worked for the Boston Consulting Group. During his career, he has led hundreds of comprehensive strategy studies for companies based in ten countries. He has also led studies for governments in Sweden, Ireland, Canada, Great Britain and Israel. Mr. Magaziner graduated from Brown University and attended Balliol College Oxford as a Rhodes Scholar. Author of numerous books, Mr. Magaziner's latest book is *The Silent War: Inside the Global Business Battles Shaping America's Future.* He is a member of the Board of Trustees of the National Center on Education and the Economy.

William E. Brock, *Co-Chair*

William E. Brock is Senior Partner of The Brock Group, a Washington, D.C. consulting firm specializing in international trade, human resources and investment strategies. Senator Brock was a member of President Reagan's Cabinet serving from 1981 to 1985 as United States Trade Representative, the President's chief trade policy adviser and international trade negotiator, and served from 1985 to 1987 as Secretary of Labor. As Secretary, he initiated the landmark study of workforce and workplace demographic trends entitled *Workforce 2000: Work and Workers for the 21st Century,* achieved major pension reform legislation and reinvigorated efforts at labor-management cooperation. Senator Brock served four terms in the House of Representatives until he was elected Senator from Tennessee in 1970. In 1977, Senator Brock served as Chairman of the Republican National Committee. Senator Brock currently serves on President Bush's Education Policy Advisory Committee, is Chairman of U. S. Labor Secretary Dole's Commission on Achieving Necessary Skills (SCANS) and is Chairman of the National Endowment for Democracy. He is also a Senior Counselor at the Center for Strategic and International Studies in Washington D.C., Chairman of the International Advisory Committee of the University of South Carolina and President of the National Academy Foundation.

Ray Marshall, *Co-Chair*

Ray Marshall holds the Audre and Bernard Rapoport Centennial Chair in Economics and Public Affairs at the L. B. J. School of Public Affairs at the University of Texas at Austin and served as President Carter's Secretary of Labor. As President Carter's chief advisor on labor matters, Mr. Marshall administered laws and programs in employment and training, labor statistics, labor-management relations and other matters affecting the nation's workforce. Mr. Marshall serves as a member of the Advisory Committee to the National Science Foundation's Directorate for Science and Engineering Education and is a member of the Boards of the American Academy of Work and Learning, the Quality Education for Minorities Network and the Interactive Training Institute. He is a Trustee of Carnegie Corporation of New York and served as a Carnegie Forum Advisory Council member. Among his recent publications is *Unheard Voices: Labor and Economic Policy in a Competitive World* (1987). Mr. Marshall is a member of the National Center's Board of Trustees.

Robert M. Atkinson, II

Director of Academic Programs for the School of Business and Industry at Florida A & M University in Tallahassee, Florida, Robert M. Atkinson is a member of the Board of Directors for the Strategic Business Investors Development Corporation where he served as Chairman of the Board from 1985 to 1987. Prior to obtaining his current position in August 1989, he was Director of the Division of Management Sciences at the School of Business and Industry from 1986 to 1989. From 1982 to 1986, he was an Associate Professor in the Division of Management Sciences. From 1974 to 1982, Mr. Atkinson was an Assistant Professor of Business Administration at the College of Commerce and Business Administration at the University of Illinois. Mr. Atkinson was a First Lieutenant in the Signal Corps, United States Army.

Owen Bieber

Owen Bieber is President of the United Automobile Workers. In 1980, he was elected International Vice President. He was elected President of the International Union first in 1983 and again in 1986. As President, Mr. Bieber has promoted greater job security for industrial workers by helping to pioneer contractual approaches, such as the creation of job banks, and has implemented a number of innovative education programs. Mr. Bieber began his career with the

UAW in 1949. He is a Vice President and an Executive Council member of the AFL-CIO and serves on the Boards of the National Association for the Advancement of Colored People, the United Way of America and New Detroit. He is a member of the Michigan Governor's Commission on Jobs and Economic Development, the Economic Alliance of Michigan and the President's Advisory Committee for Trade Negotiations.

Edward J. Carlough

Edward J. Carlough is General President of the Sheet Metal Workers' International Association, AFL-CIO. He was elected President of the union in 1970 and has been reelected without opposition at each successive convention. He has helped create the National Training Fund for apprentices and journeymen, a Stabilization Agreement to help unemployed workers and the National Energy Management Institute. Prior to becoming President, he served 13 years as the Sheet Metal Union Research Director and Organizing Director. Mr. Carlough became a Sheet Metal Workers' apprentice in New York City in 1949. Currently, he serves as Vice President of the AFL-CIO Building and Construction Trades Department and a member of the General Board of the AFL-CIO.

Anthony P. Carnevale

Anthony P. Carnevale is the Vice President of National Affairs and Chief Economist for the American Society for Training and Development (ASTD) in Alexandria, Virginia. From 1987 through 1988, Mr. Carnevale was Chairman of the Fiscal Policy Task Force for the Council on Competitiveness. From 1981 to 1982, he was co-moderator for the White House Conference on Productivity. In 1978, Mr. Carnevale served as the Government Affairs Director for the American

Federation of State, County and Municipal Employees (AFSCME). Prior to his work with AFSCME, Mr. Carnevale served in the Congress as a staff member in the U.S. House of Representatives and the Senate. Mr. Carnevale's government service also includes work in the U.S. Department of Health, Education and Welfare. Mr. Carnevale was a co-author of the principal affidavit in Rodriguez v. San Antonio, a landmark Supreme Court case arguing for equal educational opportunity. Mr. Carnevale has authored several books and monographs on training in the workplace. Mr. Carnevale holds a Ph.D. from the Maxwell School of Public Affairs of Syracuse University. He is a member of the Board of Trustees of the National Center.

Paul J. Choquette, Jr.

Paul J. Choquette, Jr. is President of Gilbane Building Company in Providence, Rhode Island. Appointed President in 1981, he is the sixth consecutive family member to serve as President since the company's founding in 1873. Before assuming his present role, Mr. Choquette served as General Counsel, Vice President and Executive Vice President at Gilbane. Currently, he also serves as Chairman of the Board of Gilbane Properties, Inc., a real estate development subsidiary of Gilbane Building Company. Mr. Choquette serves as a Trustee Emeritus of Brown University and Vice Chairman and member of the Board of Directors of the Rhode Island Port Authority and Economic Development Corporation. He is also a past Chairman of the New England Council. Prior to joining Gilbane, Mr. Choquette served as legal counsel to then Rhode Island Governor John H. Chafee for two years.

Richard Cohon

Richard Cohon is President of C.N. Burman Company in Paterson, New Jersey. Mr. Cohon also is an advisor to the President's Commission on Vocational Education. He serves as a member of the Board of Directors of the National Strategy Information Center and the United Skills Investment Corporation and is a national advisor of the Center for New Leadership. Mr. Cohon is a member of the Association for Manufacturing Excellence and the Young Presidents' Organization. He is Chairman and Founder of YPO's Manufacturing Project and Chairman of the National Center for Manufacturing Sciences' Education and Training Committee.

Badi G. Foster

Badi G. Foster is President of the AEtna Institute for Corporate Education, a position he has held since its inception in 1981. He is responsible for corporate education programs in human resources development, management, education, business strategy and organization effectiveness. Mr. Foster also oversees the Institute's management and consulting activities, educational technology and research and AEtna's educational involvement with outside organizations. Prior to joining AEtna, Mr. Foster held several positions at Harvard University including: Director of Field Experience Program, Graduate School of Education; Chairman, Hispanic Study Group; Assistant Director, J. F. Kennedy Institute of Politics; and Visiting Professor in Afro-American Studies. He has published a number of articles on business, education and community development and served in several public service capacities at the Federal, state and local government level.

Thomas Gonzales

Thomas Gonzales is Chancellor of the Seattle Community College District VI, the largest of 23 community college districts in the State of Washington. As Chancellor, he also serves as Chief Executive Officer. From 1981 to 1989, Dr. Gonzales served as President of Linn-Benton Community College in Albany, Oregon, and from

1981 to 1989 was Adjunct Professor at Oregon State University, School of Education. He was appointed by Oregon's Governor to serve on the Board of the State Apprenticeship and Training Council from 1985 to 1986. Prior to these experiences, Dr. Gonzales was Campus Vice President of the Community College of Denver, Auraria Campus, Dean of Instruction at San Jose City College and a consultant to the Wyoming Higher Education Council. Dr. Gonzales is a member of the American Association of Community and Junior Colleges (AACJC) and is Vice Chair of the AACJC Commission on Improving Minority Education. He was a former member of the AACJC Board of Directors and Chair of its membership committee. While in Oregon, Dr. Gonzales served on the Private Industry Council (PIC), and now serves on the PIC Board in Seattle, Washington.

Rear Admiral W. J. Holland, Jr., USN (Retired)

Jerry Holland is President of the Armed Forces Communications and Education Association Educational Foundation, which sponsors scholarships and provides professional training in the disciplines related to defense command, communications, intelligence, computers and information management systems. Rear Admiral Holland served on active duty for 32 years, primarily in nuclear submarines. He was a teacher and supervisor of training at every grade including command of the Navy's largest technical training facility, the Submarine School. He was the United States Naval Academy's first Director of Professional Development, a department he founded. Rear Admiral Holland has written on submarine warfare, national strategic policy, technical training and maritime affairs.

James R. Houghton

James R. Houghton is Chairman of the Board and Chief Executive Officer of Corning Incorporated. Since joining Corning in 1962, Mr. Houghton has served as European Manager, Vice President, General Manager, Director and Vice Chairman and was elected Chairman in 1983. Houghton is past Chairman of the Business Council of New York State and a member of The Business Roundtable, Council on Foreign Relations and the Business Committee for the Arts. He is also a Director of Dow Corning Corporation, Metropolitan Life Insurance Company, CBS, Inc., J.P. Morgan Company and Owens-Corning Fiberglass Corporation. He serves as a Trustee of the Corning Museum of Glass, the Corning Glass Works Foundation and the Metropolitan Museum of Art in New York City.

James B. Hunt, Jr.

James B. Hunt, Jr. served as North Carolina's first two-term Governor, holding office from 1977 to 1985. Under his leadership, the North Carolina School of Science and Mathematics, the Microelectronics Center of North Carolina and the North Carolina Business Committee for Education were all established. Governor Hunt chaired the National Governors' Association Task Force on Technological Innovation, the Education Commission of the States and its Task Force on Education for Economic Growth that produced *Action for Excellence*, one of the major education reform reports of 1983. Now an attorney in private practice with the firm of Poyner and Spruill, he was a member of the Carnegie Forum's Task Force on Teaching as a Profession, chaired the Planning Group that chartered the National Board for Professional Teaching Standards and is currently Chair of the National Board. He is also a member of the National Center's Board of Trustees.

John R. Hurley

John R. Hurley is Vice President and Director of Corporate Training and Educational Resources for The Chase Manhattan Bank. Previously, he was Director of Training at the Insurance Company of North America and has held senior level human resource and marketing positions at the Xerox Corporation. Early in his career, he was a public school teacher and school administrator. Currently, he is active on the Council for Continuing Education and is the President of the American Society for Training and Development.

John E. Jacob

John E. Jacob is President and Chief Executive Officer of the National Urban League, Inc., a position he has held since 1982. Author of a weekly newspaper column, "To Be Equal," which appears in more than 600 newspapers, Mr. Jacob has served as Executive Vice President of the National Urban League, Inc. from 1979 to 1981 and President of the Washington, D.C. Urban League from 1975 to 1979. He also acted as Executive Director of the San Diego Urban League from 1970 to 1975. Mr. Jacob began his Urban League career in 1965 as Director of Education and Youth Incentives at NUL in Washington, D.C. During his tenure, the Urban League has offered young people various workforce training, skills development and employability programs and has worked directly with school systems to improve the school-to-work transition. Mr. Jacob currently serves as Chairman of Howard University's Board of Trustees and on the Boards of Local Initiatives Support Corporation (LISC), New York Telephone, Continental Corporation and Coca-Cola Enterprises.

Thomas H. Kean

Thomas H. Kean is President of Drew University in Madison, New Jersey. Prior to assuming the presidency, he was Governor of New Jersey from 1981 to 1989. In 1987, Governor Kean chaired the Republican Governors' Association. He was a member of the Executive Committee of the National Governors' Association, Chairman of NGA's Task Force on International Education and is a member of the National Board for Professional Teaching Standards. He has also served as Chairman of the Education Commission of the States and was a member of the Carnegie Forum's Task Force on Teaching as a Profession. Before being elected Governor, Governor Kean served ten years in the New Jersey State Assembly holding positions of Minority Leader, Majority Leader and Speaker. In 1984, Governor Kean was named Man of the Year by the New Jersey NAACP. Before becoming involved in politics, he was an American history high school teacher. He is a member of the National Center's Board of Trustees.

William H. Kolberg

William H. Kolberg is President of the National Alliance of Business, a position he has held since 1980. Prior to joining the National Alliance of Business, he was Vice President for Public Affairs of the Union Camp Corporation, President of Kolberg & Associates and consultant to The Business Roundtable. Before entering private industry, he served as Assistant Secretary of Labor and Administrator of the Employment and Training Administration from 1973 to 1977. He was the Assistant Director of the Office of Management and Budget in the Executive Office of the President from 1971 to 1973. Mr. Kolberg's range of experience includes policy planning and administration, national leadership roles in employment and training, education and welfare reform and authorship of national workforce quality initiatives. In 1970, he was the recipient of the Distinguished Achievement Award of the U.S. Department of Labor. He is the author of *Preparing Manpower Legislation* and the editor of *The Dislocated Worker.*

William Lucy

William Lucy was elected International Secretary/ Treasurer, the second highest national office, of the more than one-million member American Federation of State, County and Municipal Employees (AFSCME), AFL-CIO, in 1972. A civil engineer by trade, Mr. Lucy is Vice President of the AFL-CIO Industrial Union Department, the Maritime Trades Department and the Department for Professional Employees. He serves on the Boards of the African-American Institute, Americans for Democratic Action and Commission on Working Women. He is a member of the National Leadership Conference on Civil Rights and the National Labor Advisory Council of the March of Dimes Foundation. He is President and a Founder of the Coalition of Black Trade Unionists (CBTU), an organization of union leaders and rank-and-file members dedicated to focusing on the needs of Black and minority group workers.

Margaret L.A. MacVicar

Margaret MacVicar holds the Cecil and Ida Green Chair in Education at the Massachusetts Institute of Technology, where she is Dean for Undergraduate Education and Professor of Physical Science. From 1983 to 1987, she was Vice President of the Carnegie Institution of Washington. In 1979 she was Chancellor's Distinguished Professor at the University of California at Berkeley. Dean MacVicar is Chair of the National Science Foundation's Advisory Committee on Education and Human Resources and Co-Chair of the National Council on Science and

Technology's Project 2061 of the American Association for the Advancement of Science. Professor MacVicar was a Trustee of the Carnegie Foundation for the Advancement of Teaching and a member of the Carnegie Council on Policy Studies in Higher Education. She is a member of the Corporations of Charles S. Draper Laboratory and Woods Hole Oceanographic Institution, a Trustee of Radcliffe College and the Boston Museum of Science, and a Director of Exxon Corporation and W.H. Brady Co. Dean MacVicar is a Fellow of the American Physical Society and holds patents and is published in the field of electronic materials

Eleanor Holmes Norton

Eleanor Holmes Norton, Professor of Law at the Georgetown University Law Center, was appointed by President Carter as the first woman to chair the Equal Employment Opportunity Commission. As EEOC Chair, Professor Norton administered Title VII of the 1964 Civil Rights Act, the Equal Pay Act, the Age Discrimination in Employment Act and Section 501 of the Rehabilitation Act and is highly regarded for her work in developing equal employment law and policy. Professor Norton is an authority on labor force and employment matters, anti-discrimination policy, family, education and poverty concerns. She has co-authored a book entitled *Sex Discrimination and the Law: Causes and Remedies.* She has been named one of the One Hundred Most Important Women in America, has received 53 honorary degrees and serves on the Boards of the Rockefeller Foundation, the Martin Luther King, Jr. Center for Social Change, Metropolitan Life Insurance Company, Pitney Bowes Corporation and the Stanley Works Company.

Karen Nussbaum

Karen Nussbaum is the Executive Director of 9to5, National Association of Working Women, the leading membership organization for the nation's 20 million office workers. 9to5 combines activism, research and public education to win rights and respect for women who work in offices. A former secretary herself, Ms. Nussbaum has been organizing office workers since the early 1970's and helped found one of the first 9to5 chapters in Boston in 1973. Today 9to5 has over 14,000 members with 26 chapters nationwide. She also serves as President of District 925, a national union for office workers under the Service Employees International Union, AFL-CIO. Ms. Nussbaum has co-authored *Solutions for the New Work Force: Policies for a New Social Contract* and *9to5: The Working Woman's Guide to Office Survival.*

Peter J. Pestillo

Peter J. Pestillo is Vice President of Corporate Relations and Diversified Businesses for the Ford Motor Company. He has responsibility for the Company's Employee Relations, Public Affairs and Governmental Affairs Staffs, and for Ford Aerospace Corporation and Ford New Holland, Inc. Mr. Pestillo is a member of the Board of Directors of Rouge Steel Company and Park Ridge Corporation, parent firm of Hertz Corporation. He received his law degree from Georgetown University and is a graduate of the Advanced Management Program at Harvard University.

Philip H. Power

Philip H. Power is Founder, Owner and Chairman of the Board of Suburban Communications Corporation, a group of community newspapers throughout Michigan and around Cincinnati, Ohio. Mr. Power serves on the Board of Directors of the Michigan Growth Capital Foundation, the Power Foundation, the World Press Freedom Committee and is a Trustee of the National Center on Education and the Economy. He is a member of the University of Michigan's Board of Regents, chairs the Michigan Job Training Coordinating Council and is a member of Governor Blanchard's Cabinet Council on Human Investment and Commission on Jobs and Economic Development. Mr. Power is widely recognized for his highly regarded reorganization of Michigan's job training programs, as well as for his development of an integrated labor market policy for the state.

Lauren B. Resnick

Lauren B. Resnick is Director of the Learning Research and Development Center and Professor of Psychology and Education at the University of Pittsburgh. In 1986, Professor Resnick was President of the American Educational Research Association and from 1979 to 1980 was President of the American Psychological Association's Division of Educational Psychology. She has been a member of the National Research Council's Commission on Behavioral and Social Sciences and Education, the Board of Trustees of the Carnegie Foundation for the Advancement of Teaching and the Educational Testing Service. Ms. Resnick currently serves on the Mathematical Sciences Education Board and on U. S. Labor Secretary Dole's Commission on Achieving Necessary Skills (SCANS). Professor Resnick is the founder and editor of *Cognition and Instruction.* She is a member of the Board of Trustees of the National Center.

Kjell-Jon Rye

Kjell-Jon Rye is a teacher at Bellevue High School in Bellevue, Washington. A teacher in this school since 1984, Mr. Rye established the Technology Education Program, which includes instruction in the following areas: robotics, lasers, computers, aerospace and biomedical technology, construction, manufacturing, communications and transportation technology and mechanical, electronic, architectural and civil engineering. He is an advisor to the Congressional Office of Technology Assessment on issues relating to technology and education of youth. Mr. Rye was a member of the Washington State Advanced Technology Advisory Board, which advised the Governor on policies relating to the impacts of advanced technology on education. He is currently a member of the Technology Education Advisory Council of the International Technology Education Association and sits on the Editorial Board of Educational Digest. He is currently on leave at the Center for Educational Renewal at the University of Washington working with Dr. John I. Goodlad.

Howard D. Samuel

Howard D. Samuel is currently President of the Industrial Union Department, a semi-autonomous organization associated with the AFL-CIO. He has had a forty-year career in the labor movement. Prior to his role at IUD, Mr. Samuel was Deputy Under Secretary of Labor for International Affairs. In that position, he directed the Labor Department's Bureau of International Labor Affairs and was responsible for international activities. Mr. Samuel has served on various commissions including: the National Manpower Advisory Council, the Commission on Population Growth and the American Future and the President's Commission on Competitiveness. He

serves as Trustee of the Brookings Institution, Martin Luther King Center, Work in America Institute and the Council on Competitiveness and is a member of the Defense Science Board.

John Sculley

John Sculley joined Apple Computer, Inc. as President and Chief Executive Officer in 1983 and was elected Chairman of the Board in 1986. Mr. Sculley has led Apple to a top position in the personal computer industry, focusing on technology for business and education. Prior to joining Apple, Mr. Sculley was President and Chief Executive Officer of Pepsi-Cola Company. He is the recipient of numerous awards, including Advertising Man of the Year, the Joseph E. Wharton Business-Statesman Leadership Award and UCLA's Anderson Graduate School of Management Exemplary Leadership in Management Award. Most recently, he was chosen CEO of the Decade for Marketing by the Financial News Network. Mr. Sculley serves on the Board of the international Foundation for the Survival and Development of Humanity, an East-West cooperative effort on human rights, education, arms reduction, energy and the environment. He also serves on the SEI Board at the Center for Advanced Studies and Management and on the Board of Overseers, both at the Wharton School, on the Board of Advisors at the Graduate School of Business at Stanford University and on the Board of Trustees at Brown University. Mr. Sculley is the author of the best selling autobiography, *Odyssey, Pepsi to Apple.* Mr. Sculley serves as the Chairman of the National Center's Board of Trustees.

William J. Spring

Since 1984, William J. Spring has been the Vice President of District Community Affairs at the Federal Reserve Bank of Boston. Prior to his current role, Mr. Spring was a consultant to the Federal Reserve Bank of Boston and President of the Boston Private Industry Council from 1983 to 1985 where he was extensively involved in setting up the Boston Compact. From 1977 through 1981, Mr. Spring was the Associate Director for Employment Policy with the Domestic Policy Staff at the White House. He is the author and co-author of numerous articles on employment policy as seen in *The New York Times Magazine, The New Republic, The Washington Post* and *The Boston Globe*. Mr. Spring authored a working paper for the National Center entitled, "From 'Solution' to Catalyst: A New Role for Federal Education and Training Dollars."

Anthony J. Trujillo

Anthony J. Trujillo is Superintendent of the Sweetwater Union High School District in Chula Vista, California. Prior to becoming a Superintendent, Mr. Trujillo was a teacher, principal and administrator and has taught at the university level. Mr. Trujillo served as Chairman of the Educational Management and Evaluation Commission for the California State Board of Education from 1978 to 1980 and Chairman of the State Commission on School Governance and Management from 1984 to 1985. Currently, he is a member of the San Diego United Way Board of Directors.

Marc S. Tucker

Marc S. Tucker is President of the National Center on Education and the Economy. He was principal author of the Center's report, *To Secure Our Future: The Federal Role In Education.* Prior to the establishment of the National Center in January 1988, he was Executive Director of the Carnegie Forum on Education and the Economy.

Mr. Tucker served as Staff Director and principal author for the Forum's report, *A Nation Prepared: Teachers for the 21st Century.* Mr. Tucker serves as a member of the Board of Visitors of the College and Graduate School of Arts and Sciences at Wake Forest University, the Board of Visitors of the University of Pittsburgh's School of Education and the Board of Directors of the National Alliance of Business Center for Excellence in Education. Mr. Tucker is also a Professor of Education at the University of Rochester.

Laura D'Andrea Tyson

Laura D'Andrea Tyson is Director of Research at the Berkeley Roundtable on the International Economy (BRIE) and Professor of Economics at the University of California at Berkeley. She was a visiting professor at Harvard Business School during the 1989 to 1990 academic year. Prior to joining the faculty at the University of California, she was an Assistant Professor of Economics at Princeton University. She is a member of the Cuomo Commission on Trade and Competitiveness, the Leadership Council of Rebuild America and the Council on Foreign Relations. She has served as a consultant to the President's Commission on Industrial Competitiveness, Council on Competitiveness, Western Governors' Association, World Bank, the Office of Technology Assessment and RAND Corporation. Ms. Tyson has written numerous books on the economics of competitiveness including: *American Industry in International Competition* (1983), *The Dynamics of Trade and Employment* (1988) and *Politics and Productivity: The Real Story of How Japan Works* (1989). She is currently working on a book on trade policy for the Institute of International Economics in Washington, D.C.

Kay R. Whitmore

Kay R. Whitmore is Chairman, President, and Chief Executive Officer of Eastman Kodak Company in Rochester, New York. He began his career at Kodak as an engineer in film manufacturing in 1957. Mr. Whitmore serves as a member of the Board of Directors of The Chase Manhattan Corporation, The Business Roundtable, the Business Council of the State of New York, the University of Rochester and the International Museum of Photography at the George Eastman House. He is Chairman of the Industrial Management Council of Rochester. He is also a member of the National Center's Board of Trustees.

Alan L. Wurtzel

Alan L. Wurtzel is Chairman of the Board and former Chief Executive Officer of Circuit City Stores. Under his leadership, Circuit City has become the largest and most profitable specialty retailer of brand-name consumer electronics and appliances in the United States with sales in excess of $2 billion. Prior to joining Circuit City Stores, Mr. Wurtzel was a Washington, D.C. attorney. From 1986 to 1988, Mr. Wurtzel served as President of Operation Independence, a nonprofit organization whose goal is to assist Israel to become economically independent. Currently he serves as a member of the Board of Visitors of Virginia Commonwealth University, Trustee of Oberlin College, Director of Office Depot (the nation's largest office speciality retail store chain), Washington Project for the Arts and the Greater Washington Educational Telecommunications Association, which operates the public radio and television stations in Washington, D.C.

COMMISSION ON THE SKILLS OF THE AMERICAN WORKFORCE
COMMISSION ASSOCIATES

David J. Barram
Vice President
Corporate Affairs
Apple Computer, Inc.

Eugene C. Baten
Consultant
AEtna Institute for Corporate Education

Ellen Bravo
Associate Director
9to5, National Association of Working Women

Renee S. Lerche
Education Projects Development Manager
Ford Motor Company

David Luther
Senior Vice President, Corporate
  Director-Quality
Corning Incorporated

John R. McCarthy
Senior Vice President and Director
Corporate Relations
Eastman Kodak Company

Frank Musick
Director
Special Projects
United Automobile Workers

Stephanie G. Robinson
Director
Education and Career Development
National Urban League, Inc.

Freeman Smith
Director
State and Local Government Relations
Corning Incorporated

Billy J. Tidwell
Director of Research
Washington Operations
National Urban League, Inc.

James D. Van Erden
Administrator
Office of Work-Based Learning
U.S. Department of Labor

COMMISSION ON THE SKILLS OF THE AMERICAN WORKFORCE
CASE STUDY RESEARCH TEAM AND STAFF

Apple Computer, Inc.
Lucille Ueltzen
Manager, Apple University Operations

Center for the Study of Human Resources
University of Texas at Austin
Robert Glover
Research Associate

The Chase Manhattan Bank
Charlotte Pollard
Vice President, Learning Resources

Laura Coyne
Second Vice President, Learning Resources

Cresap, a Towers Perrin company
Eugene R. Smoley, Jr.
Vice President

Eastman Kodak Company
Susan Connolly
Director of Education Development

Dennis Lyons
Director of Technical Education Resources

International Brotherhood of Electrical
Workers
Ken Edwards
Director of Technical Training

National Alliance of Business
Betsy Brown Ruzzi
Senior Project Manager, Youth and Education
Programs

Pete Carlson
Director, Economic and Policy Analysis

National Center on Education
and the Economy
Joan L. Wills, *Project Manager*
Vice President

Jana L. Carlisle
Staff Associate

Tina Isaacs
Staff Associate

Larry A. McKnight
Network Administrator

Ann Marie Potter
Staff Assistant

Patrina Smith
Administrative Assistant

Cathy D. Spangenburg
Staff Assistant

Susan Sullivan
Director, Administrative Services

Sheet Metal Workers' International Association

Jerry Olejniczak
Administrator, National Training Fund

Palmer C. Pilcher
Consultant

SJS, Inc.

Karen Barajas
Associate

Sarah H. Cleveland
Associate

Christine Heenan
Associate

Sean Rocha
Associate

Marjorie Tarmey
Associate

Chip Young
Associate

Telesis/Cresap, a Towers Perrin company

Edward J. Caron, *Case Study Team Coordinator*
Managing Consultant

Stephen W. Coon
Consultant

Cynthia Isabella
Administrative Assistant

Lynn M. Margherio
Research Associate

William J. Maroni
Consultant

Debra Morris
Administrative Assistant

Norene M. Rickson
Consultant

Denise Ricketson
Administrative Assistant

Deborah Rosen
Research Associate

TPF&C, a Towers Perrin company

Karl F. Price
Principal

United Automobile Workers/Chrysler National Training Center

Linell Burrell, Jr.
Grant and Training Specialist

U.S. Department of Labor

Ambrose "Red" Bittner
Chief of National Program Coordination
   and Training Group
Bureau of Apprenticeship and Training

Janet Pease Moore
Executive Assistant
Office of Work-Based Learning

Publications Order Form

National Center on Education and the Economy Publications	Quantity	Cost

Commission on the Skills of the American Workforce
America's Choice: high skills or low wages!
  The Report of the Commission on the Skills of the American Workforce
  ISBN 0-9627063-0-2
    1-9 copies $18.00 each ppd.
    10+ $15.00 each ppd.

America's Choice: high skills or low wages!
Supporting Works
  (Documents the Commission's international, labor market and industry research)
  Commission on the Skills of the American Workforce
  $45 each ppd.

Federal Role Series
To Secure Our Future: The Federal Role in Education
  National Center on Education and the Economy
  $7.50 each ppd.

Commissioned Papers - $4.00 each ppd.
The Yoke of Special Education: How To Break It
  Alan Gartner and Dorothy Kerzner Lipsky

Training America: Strategies for the Nation
  Anthony P. Carnevale and Janet Johnston

Higher Education and American Competitiveness
  Ernest A. Lynton

From "Solution" to Catalyst: A New Role for Federal Education
and Training Dollars
  William J. Spring

Also Available

A Nation Prepared: Teachers for the 21st Century
  The Report of the Taskforce on Teaching as a Profession for the
  Carnegie Forum on Education and the Economy
  ISBN 0-9616685-0-4
    1-10 copies $9.95 each ppd.
    11-25 $8.95 each ppd.
    26 + $6.95 each ppd.

               TOTAL: _____

Please complete the following:

Purchase Order #: _____

Name: _____

Title: _____

Institution: _____

_____

Address: _____

_____

City: _____

State: _____ Zip: _____

Telephone: ( ) _____

Please make purchase order or
check payable to:

National Center on Education
 and the Economy

Send orders to:
National Center on Education
 and the Economy
P.O. Box 10670
Rochester, New York 14610

• All orders must be prepaid by
check or accompanied by a
purchase order.
• Allow 4 - 6 weeks for delivery.
• No refunds for overstock.